MW00900069

MARY'S
CALL TO PRAYER

The Mother of Jesus Speaks

JOHN D. SMATLAK

WestBow Press books may be ordered through booksellers or by contacting:

WestBow Press
A Division of Thomas Nelson & Zondervan
1663 Liberty Drive
Bloomington, IN 47403
www.westbowpress.com
844-714-3454

ISBN: 978-1-6642-1542-9 (sc)
ISBN: 978-1-6642-1544-3 (hc)
ISBN: 978-1-6642-1543-6 (e)

Library of Congress Control Number: 2020924082

Print information available on the last page.

WestBow Press rev. date: 01/13/2021

This book is dedicated to my children, who live with faith in Christ.

I deeply appreciate the advice and encouragement given by friends, family members, and clergy.

John Smatlak

CONTENTS

FOREWORD

One day soon, every individual will simultaneously experience an illumination of conscience. It will be seen and felt interiorly by each person in the world, including atheists and people of all religions. Everyone will know it is from God and that God is real. In an illumination of conscience, people will see the wrong they have done and the good they have failed to do. They will see themselves as God sees them. It is meant to purify people and correct the conscience of the world. This will be a time of divine mercy. Many will convert and confess their sins. Some individuals may die from being horrified at seeing themselves through the eyes of God. Some atheists will convert, but others will continue to hate God.

PREFACE

The Roman Catholic Church and the Coptic Orthodox Church, based in Egypt, accept as "worthy of belief" thirty-four sites in the world where Mary, the mother of Jesus, returned to earth in an apparition, a supernatural appearance of a person or thing. Over multiple centuries, visionaries have reported seeing and speaking with Mary. Nearly all apparition events include evidence of other miracles.

There are distinctions made in the level of approval for each of the thirty-four sites, which are determined by the following: Vatican approved, Coptic Church approved, local bishop approved, authentic miracle with implied approval of the apparition, approved for veneration (to regard with reverence and respect), and approved for pilgrimage.

An apparition is more of a physical nature, while a vision is more of a spiritual nature. The Catholic Church believes that many claimed apparitions are fabricated by the visionary or the result of something other than divine intervention. For this reason, there is a formal evaluation process established to assess claimed apparitions. A bishop establishes a commission of experts, including theologians, psychologists, and doctors, to determine and verify the facts. Visionaries and witnesses of the apparition are required to participate in a thorough examination with questions verifying their credibility.

Apparitions are evaluated on many criteria, including the sincerity and moral uprightness of the visionaries, the theological accuracy of the divine messages, and positive spiritual fruits resulting from the apparition event. This often includes evidence of miraculous healings and conversions to the Christian faith.

Once the Catholic Church approves an apparition, belief in the apparition is never required of Catholic parishioners. Catholic faith is rooted in public revelation, which ended with the death of the last living apostle, John. A Marian apparition is considered a private revelation. It may emphasize some facet of public revelation for a specific purpose. However, it can never add anything new to the deposit of faith, the body of revealed truth in the scriptures, and tradition proposed by the Roman Catholic Church for the belief of the faithful. Approved Marian apparitions are representative of Mary's evangelical mission, which is to show the way to the Father's house through faith in Jesus.

In the Catholic Church, approval of a Marian apparition is rare. Most investigated apparition claims are rejected as fraudulent or false. Some apparition claims found to be false result in a claimant's break from the Catholic Church to form their own splinter church.

Of the thirty-four Marian apparitions, eighteen are summarized in this book. Six are Vatican approved. One is approved by the Coptic Church. Eight are approved by a local bishop. One has implied approval. One is approved for veneration. One is approved for pilgrimage.

Mary's primary message in the apparitions is a call to prayer. It is intended for all Christians to hear, not just for Catholics and Coptic Orthodox. Mary tells Protestants, Anglicans, Catholics, and Orthodox there is an insufficient amount of prayer in the world. The time for every Christian to pray more is now.

INTRODUCTION

Mary, the mother of Jesus, is a relatively new source of information about Christianity. She is an untapped resource containing twentieth-century news about religion. Mary miraculously appears to people on earth in many different countries. During these apparition visits, she sends us messages. It is through these messages, given directly to a few chosen people who personally meet with her, that Mary gives the world new and recent information from heaven and her Son, Jesus.

The Bible is the foremost and best source of information about Christianity, Jesus, and the early church. Spiritual understanding can be enriched by reading the works of early church fathers, such as St. Augustine and Thomas Aquinas. Modern books, such as those written by C. S. Lewis, Pope John Paul II, and other men and women of God, provide even more enlightenment. However, Mary answers many of the questions people are asking today.

The New Testament Gospel of Luke tells us Mary is the virgin mother of Jesus, who will be called "blessed" across all generations (Luke 1:34, 48). While some of Mary's apparition sites are visited by tens of millions of people every year, much of the world population is unaware of her miraculous interventions.

There are books and articles written about each individual apparition site. However, a summary of Mary's visits and her messages are included in this book. A chronological list of Marian visitations may surprise Christians with its number of occurrences and timeline.

After reading a summary of influential Marian apparitions, similar key messages from these divine experiences become more apparent.

Mary accurately predicts future events on earth. Evidence of God's supernatural abilities are displayed by many miracle healings at Mary's visitation sites. At Mary's request, God makes the sun dance for thousands to see and understand his power.

Mary's primary message is a call to prayer. She repeats this message at every visitation site. Christians have the power of prayer to convert atheists and to stop wars. However, Christians increasingly fail to use this power. Denial of God is widespread, and war seems to never end. More prayer is the solution.

Mary directly answers questions, like, what does it take to get to heaven, and what behaviors cause a person to go to hell. You gain a better understanding of Jesus, Mary, and other supernatural beings. You learn from Mary what is important to gain eternal life—and what is not. Mary communicates clear expectations for Christians on earth. She expresses her deep love for people, warns of dire future events on earth, and explains how to either mitigate or avoid the dire events with prayer.

In perfect alignment with the Bible and Jesus, Mary speaks to us today.

CHAPTER 1
LIFE AFTER THIS LIFE

> Our Lady [Mary] gave a great gift to me, but also a great gift to the world, because all of us ask ourselves, is there life after this life. I'm standing here before all of you as a living witness, and I can tell you, *there is a life after this life*; because on that day in May [1985] I was able to see my late mother. I was able to give her a hug, and my mother told me, *my child I am proud of you.*
>
> —Ivanka Ivankovic

Visionary Ivanka Ivankovic is from Medjugorje (pronounced Med-ju-gory) in the country of Bosnia and Herzegovina (part of the former Yugoslavia). She spoke about meeting loved ones in the afterlife. Ivanka is one of six visionaries in Medjugorje who regularly meet and speak with Mary, the mother of Jesus.

When Mary appears, she comes as a supernatural apparition and often meets with all six visionaries together. However, there are times when Mary meets individually with each visionary. Mary communicates messages from heaven and her Son, Jesus, to the world through these six visionaries.

In her messages, Mary literally refers to living people on earth as "travelers." They are traveling on a journey in transition from this world of reality to the eternal spiritual world. Mary told Ivanka, "Do not forget that you are travelers on the way to eternity. Because time on earth is so short, do not bind yourselves to material things, but to God. Your life is as passing as a flower."

Mary said, "You go to heaven in full conscience—that which you have now. In the moment of death, you are conscious of the separation of the body and soul. It is false to teach people that you are reborn many times and that you pass to different bodies. One is born only once. The body, drawn from earth, decomposes after death; it never comes back to life again. Humans receive a transfigured body."

HEAVEN AND HELL REALLY DO EXIST

In the ongoing apparitions with the Medjugorje visionaries, Mary is often sorrowful and sometimes crying. She knows in her heart what happens to the souls of atheists if they do not reconcile with God. They end up in the fires of hell for eternity. Mary often appears on earth to communicate messages specifically to atheists. She requests prayers from the faithful for those who do not believe in God. Mary desperately wants atheists to convert before it is too late.

Marija Pavlovic is another Medjugorje visionary. Mary told Marija that there are many people who do not believe there is a heaven or hell. It is most important for them to understand that heaven and hell truly exist. Life on earth passes like a flower. Eternal life does not pass; it is forever. Mary urges everyone to think more about the spiritual life and of paradise while on earth.

A TRANSITION FROM TIME TO ETERNITY

Mary said her Son, as God, looks "above" time. However, Mary, with help from her Son, can see "in" time. When people pass from "life on earth" to "life in eternity," they pass from "time" to "eternity."

Earthly life is scheduled. There is an end point to life, a certain number of years. There is a time to be a child after birth. Then there is time for young adulthood, followed by the working years. Retirement and aging are normally the final stages of life.

Time is used to segment and organize different periods of earthly life to help us manage better. It is beneficial only because there is a finite life span. In eternity, people live forever and do not age. So there is no need or benefit to tracking time.

In the moment of death, people begin a transition from "time" to "eternity." How people live during time determines where they spend eternity: either in heaven or in hell.

CHAPTER 2

Do You Believe in Miracles?

Thomas Aquinas was a Dominican friar, philosopher, Christian priest, and theologian. He was born in Lazio, Italy, in 1225. He studied in Naples and Paris and taught in Cologne, Paris, and Rome. He wrote extensive commentaries on the Bible and Christian beliefs. Because Aquinas lived during the thirteenth century, there was only one version of the Christian religion. He lived several hundred years before Christianity separated into Protestantism and Catholicism. Fifty years after his death, Thomas Aquinas was canonized as a saint in the Christian church. Saint Thomas Aquinas is considered one of the church's greatest theologians and philosophers. His writings are still used today to help train those studying for the priesthood.

Thomas Aquinas once said, "To one who has faith, no explanation is necessary. To one without faith, no explanation is possible." As for miracles, Aquinas also claimed that one cannot believe by faith and know by rational demonstration the very same truth since this would make one or the other kind of knowledge superfluous. In other words, if you have scientific evidence that proves an event was a miracle, you cannot also believe by faith that it was a miracle. For believers in Christ, everything is possible. For nonbelievers, there are many limitations.

Miracles are what Jesus used to spread Christianity while he was on earth. Jesus taught his disciples to perform miracles with the power of the Holy Spirit. After Jesus ascended to heaven, he left behind the Holy Spirit for Christians to continue performing miracles. The disciples taught other early church leaders to perform miracles as Christianity spread farther into the world.

WHAT THE NEW TESTAMENT TELLS US ABOUT MIRACLES

In the four Gospels of the Bible's New Testament, we learn that Jesus performed many miracles of healing. Jesus restored sight, healed the sick, healed a paralyzed servant, healed a man's withered hand, healed a deaf man, healed a cripple, cast out demons, replaced an ear that was cut off, and raised people from the dead. People who exhibited faith in the power of Jesus were healed of physical afflictions. Faith was the only requirement.

Jesus sometimes used soil or water to assist in the miracle of healing. When healing a man who was blind from birth, Jesus mixed spit with soil and placed the mud on the man's eyes. Jesus then told the man to go and wash in the pool of Siloam. When healing a man who was deaf and mute, Jesus first touched the man's ears and then spit on his own hand. Jesus then proceeded to use his fingers to touch some of the spit and place it on the man's tongue.

Jesus also performed many miracles that did not involve healing. He was born to a virgin, turned water into wine, walked on water, fed five thousand people with only two loaves of bread and five fish, filled a fishing net bursting full of fish, helped Peter catch a fish with a coin in its mouth, calmed a storm, met with people after being resurrected from the dead, and ascended into heaven.

On the day of Pentecost, the Holy Spirit descended with a rush of air and filled the disciples with divine power. They spoke to an international crowd, yet they were able to speak the language of each nation, allowing everyone to hear and understand in their own language. Peter preached to a crowd of Jewish men who saw the language miracle. When he finished preaching, three thousand people converted to Christianity. Later, Peter healed a man who had been lame since birth, and another two thousand people converted to Christ.

APPARITIONS IN THE BIBLE

Apparitions occurred during the time when Jesus used miracles to expand Christianity to new believers. Jesus arranged for three apostles to meet with apparitions of Moses and Elijah on top of a mountain, more commonly called the Transfiguration. God the Father spoke directly to those three apostles as they met with the apparitions.

An angel met with Mary to announce the virgin birth of Jesus. An angel spoke to Joseph in a dream. An angel met with Zechariah to announce the birth of his son, John the Baptist. The Spirit of God descended like a dove after Jesus was baptized, and then God the Father spoke directly to humans. An angel rolled the stone away from the tomb of Jesus and spoke to Mary Magdalene.

WHAT CHRISTIANS BELIEVE

Christians believe in miracles. Christians believe God's power is unlimited. According to Jesus and his disciples, miracles of healing are one of the signs that a church is a true Christian church. However, Christians more readily believe in miracles where someone is healed of a physical affliction.

They believe a lame person can miraculously walk again. They believe someone with cancer can be miraculously healed through prayer. They believe blind people can regain their sight through the miracle of prayer. They believe someone with deafness can hear again.

WHAT NON-CHRISTIANS BELIEVE

Skeptics can easily rationalize a miracle. They can readily develop a way to explain a miraculous event as nonmiraculous, rational, and repeatable. It is a question of what limits they place on God's power.

LIMITATIONS ON A CHRISTIAN BELIEF IN MIRACLES

Some Christians are less comfortable about believing in miracles where a person from the Bible comes back from heaven in a way that you can see them and speak with them, commonly called an apparition. If an apparition of Moses or Elijah appeared today, most Christians would be skeptical. Many Protestants are uncomfortable about believing in miracles where Mary, the mother of Jesus, appears and speaks. They were taught to show minimal devotion or divine respect for Mary.

Some Christians are uncomfortable with using holy water or holy soil from sacred sites when praying for a miracle. They may feel that prayer, by itself, is enough to request a miracle from God. Nothing else is needed.

Other Christians are uncomfortable with the idea that God can move objects around. In the stories of Marian apparitions, God makes the sun dance. God also drops rose petals from the sky. Some Christians may believe there are other earthly explanations for both situations. However, all miracles in Marian apparitions are consistent with miracles from the New Testament.

MARY'S APPARITION SITES

Each year, tens of millions of Christians visit Marian apparition sites. Miracle healings occur there. Many Christian believers make an annual pilgrimage walk to these sites where miracles occur, just to be closer to God.

However, most Christians are unaware of these miracles and

these sites. Their experiences with miracles and with God are unfairly restricted. As a result, many Protestants and Catholics miss the full experience of God's grace.

An ability to believe in both Catholic and Protestant miracles is affected by many life experiences, including the church in which you were raised; any religious bias you were taught by your parents; your understanding of the history of Christianity and Protestantism; and your exposure to different worship practices within the Christian religion. Whether you are Protestant or Catholic, reading about Mary's apparition messages provides a perfect opportunity to broaden your understanding of Christianity.

MISSING MAJOR CHRISTIAN EVENTS

Many Christians privately wish they could have lived during the time of Jesus. There is an allure to meeting Jesus, hearing him speak, and seeing his miracles firsthand. Christians may believe there was an advantage to living during that time, instead of living in the twentieth-century. They forget that most people did not believe in Jesus, even as he lived in their midst.

Today, Mary visits earth from heaven and gives the world messages from her Son, Jesus. God performs many miracles at the sites of Mary's apparitions. Mary even gives people in today's world a glimpse of heaven and hell. However, just as in the time of Jesus, most people do not believe Mary is in their midst.

CHAPTER 3
The Holy House in Loreto, Italy

The Church of the Annunciation in Nazareth, Israel, is a two-story basilica constructed in 1969. It was built over the foundation that remains from the house of the Virgin Mary, where Jesus was raised. Like many holy Christian sites in Israel, a Catholic church was typically built over a holy site to protect and preserve it.

The site of the Church of the Annunciation is where Mary was conceived and born. It is the site where archangel Gabriel told Mary, while in her teenage years, that she would become the mother of the Son of God. It is the place where Mary responded by saying, "May it be done to me according to your word" (Luke 1:38). It is the place where the Holy Family lived and where Jesus learned the carpentry trade. It is the location where "the Word became flesh" (John 1:14).

After Christ's ascension during apostolic times, a tradition of using the Holy House as a place of worship and pilgrimage began. Peter may have celebrated his first Holy Communion after the resurrection of Christ at that site. The house and grotto formed part of the crypt of a new church. Around the year 313, Constantine the Great constructed a large basilica around the Holy House. It was later destroyed.

The foundation of the Holy House is in Nazareth. However, the actual Holy House itself is now located in Loreto, Italy, which is about two thousand miles away.

ANGELS FLY THE HOLY HOUSE ACROSS THE SEA

In the thirteenth century, Jerusalem was under siege and about to fall to the Turks during the Crusades, a religious war between Christians and Muslims. In order to save the Holy House from being destroyed, angels transported it across the Mediterranean Sea from Nazareth to Croatia on May 10, 1291. The Blessed Virgin Mary appeared in Croatia near the house, and many miracles were reported. Several years later, on December 10, 1294, after Muslims invaded Albania, angels again transported the Holy House across the Adriatic Sea to eastern Italy.

The Holy House is thirty-one feet long by thirteen feet wide, and it has no foundation. It is made of stone and bricks. The dimensions of the Loreto house match perfectly with the dimensions of the foundation in Nazareth. The style of cuts in the stones of the house in Loreto match with cuts in the stones found in houses in Nazareth, not in Italy. The stones and brick are indigenous to Nazareth and are not found anywhere in Italy. The chemical composition of the mortar holding the stones and brick together in the house in Loreto match the chemical composition of mortar found near Nazareth, not in Italy. Inscribed words using a mix of Hebrew letters and Greek characters in the Loreto house match inscribed words in the Nazareth foundation.

Professor Giorgio Nicolini devoted his life to the study and research of the Holy House in Loreto. He researched historical, documentary, archaeological, and scientific evidence. He reviewed eyewitness accounts of those who saw the house in the air and of those who saw evidence of miracles.

Professor Nicolini established a chronology of events to help with the investigation. Eyewitnesses confirmed the Holy House was in Nazareth on May 9, 1291. On the night of May 9 to May 10, 1291, the house traveled two thousand miles to Trsat, Croatia. Nicolo Frangipane, feudal lord of Trsat sent a delegation to Nazareth to see if the Holy House was missing. The delegation confirmed the house was missing, but the foundation remained.

In Trsat, the pastor of the Church of St. George, Alexander Georgevich, was surprised by the sudden presence of the small building. He prayed for understanding. The Blessed Virgin Mary appeared to him in his sleep and told him the building was the Holy House of Nazareth, and it was brought to Trsat through the power of God. In order to confirm what Mary was telling Father Alexander, an illness from which he suffered for many years was immediately healed.

More than three years later, on the night of December 9 to 10, 1294, the Holy House disappeared from Trsat and appeared in Posatora, Italy. A church was constructed on the Posatora site as a memorial. The time and date of the Holy House there was confirmed with a signature of the local priest, Don Matteo. Two tombstones also commemorate the date of the occurrence.

ANGELS FLY THE HOLY HOUSE TO LORETO, ITALY

After nine months in Posatora, the Holy House moved to a forest that belonged to a woman named Loreta, near the town of Recanati, Italy. That is where the name Loreto came from. Between 1295 and 1296, after eight months near Recanati, the house was transported to a farm on Mount Prodo. In 1296, after six months on the farm, the house was transported to its current location: a public road on Mount Prodo connecting Recanati to Ancona. A basilica was constructed over the Holy House at its current location in Loreto to protect and preserve it.

Three churches were built in Ancona to commemorate the eyewitness accounts of those seeing the Holy House flying in the night sky. Some fishermen also reported their eyewitness accounts of seeing the Holy House flying. A memorial basilica, dedicated to "Santa Maria di Loreto," was constructed in Forio, on Ischia Island, to commemorate what the fishermen saw in 1295.

Professor Nicolini postulated that if the house had been dismantled and rebuilt, it could not possibly maintain the exact proportions of the foundation in Nazareth. Nor was it possible for the house to be dismantled or rebuilt without someone seeing or hearing it, especially over the span of one night. Even more inexplicable is the fact that the house came to its final location on a dirt highway that was used regularly by carriages and herding animals.

Nicolini estimated the stone house would weigh a few tons. Transport of the dismantled house by road would have been unfeasible due to the delay in gathering the necessary chariots, animals, and men. While transportation by sea would have been more feasible, it would be time-consuming, and the risk of storms would be too great.

Professor Nicolini concluded that for human hands to move the Holy House two thousand miles, it would have been even more miraculous than the work of angels. It is much more reasonable to conclude it was the work of angels, through the power of God. With God, nothing is impossible. He has performed greater miracles.

The Holy House in Loreto was visited by philosopher Descartes, writer Montaigne, kings, popes, and millions of pilgrims. Mozart played the organ in its church. Christopher Columbus made a vow to the Madonna of Loreto in 1493 while at sea during a storm. Napoleon plundered the shrine in 1797. He took precious jewels, which were gifts from French monarchs and European aristocracy, but he left the house undamaged.

MANY HEALING MIRACLES STILL OCCUR

The most treasured and venerated shrine to the Blessed Virgin Mary in the world is the Holy House of Loreto. Unlike other Catholic shrines, the Holy House of Loreto is under the direct authority and protection of the pope. So many miracles of healing occur at the Holy House in Loreto that they are no longer recorded. More than two thousand people who were canonized, beatified, or made venerable by the Catholic Church visited the Holy House. Four million people visit the Holy House each year.

The site in Croatia where Mary appeared was never officially investigated as a potential apparition site. Mary appeared there in a vision, not an apparition. However, the Holy House in Loreto serves as an example of Mary's supernatural intervention on earth and a precursor to future interventions.

Pope John Paul II visited the Holy House in Loreto five times. He called it "the house of all God's adopted children." He said, "The threads of history of the whole of humanity are tied anew in that house. It is the shrine of the house of Nazareth, to which the church that is in Italy is tied by providence, that the latter rediscovers a quickening reminder of the mystery of the Incarnation, thanks to which each person is called to the dignity of the Son of God."

CHAPTER 4
THE CATHOLIC VIEW OF MARY

In Palestine, during the time of Jesus, women were treated with very little respect. Each morning, Jewish men would typically recite a prayer thanking God they were not a Gentile, a slave, or a woman. Luke, the only Gospel writer who was a Gentile, was probably from Macedonia, where women were held in higher esteem. Luke writes about the birth of Jesus from Mary's point of view. He describes the roles of different women in the life of Jesus more vividly than other Gospels. Although little was written about Mary in the New Testament, the Gospel of Luke provides more information than any other Gospel.

In the Bible's Gospel of Luke, we learn archangel Gabriel shows Mary great honor by saying she has "found favor with God" (Luke 1:30). Elizabeth, mother of John the Baptist and a relative of Mary (Luke 1:36), tells Mary, "Blessed are you among women" (Luke 1:42). Mary also prophesized in the Gospel of Luke that all generations will call her "blessed" (Luke 1:48). This is the biblical basis on which the Catholic Church honors the Blessed Virgin Mary.

Mary and Joseph raised Jesus from infancy. When her Son was an adult, Mary stood at the foot of the cross where he was hung and watched while he was crucified to save humanity. She suffered great anguish while watching her Son slowly die an excruciatingly painful death.

Jesus is hanging on the cross greatly suffering as he tells John, his beloved disciple, that Mary is now John's mother. Jesus then tells Mary that John is now her son, the one who will take care of her (John 19:26–27). John took Mary to his home to live, as though she was his own mother.

THE QUEEN'S INTERCESSION

In Revelation 12:1, it says that a great sign appeared in heaven: a woman clothed with the sun, with the moon under her feet, and a crown of twelve stars on her head. Catholics interpret this to mean Mary is the queen of heaven. In Gospel times, a king was typically a man. The king's mother reigned as queen, not the king's wife.

The intercession of Mary, a king's mother, is shown in the Bible to be influential. At Mary's request, Jesus performed his first miracle of turning water into wine at a wedding in Cana. At first, Jesus responded to Mary that it was not his appointed time to perform miracles. Mary interceded persistently and Jesus reluctantly performed the miracle. Mary, the king's mother, intercedes on behalf of others with her Son, Jesus, to influence him to do things he would not otherwise do.

ISLAM RESPECTS MARY

Mary is an important figure in the Islamic religion. She is mentioned in the Koran thirty-four times, either directly or indirectly. Mary is the only woman mentioned in the Koran, and there is even an entire chapter named for her. Mary is revered in Islam for her purity and virginity. Her nature is considered exempt from all sin. It is an Islamic belief that God predestined Mary and purified her, raising her above all women.

DOGMAS OF THE CATHOLIC CHURCH

A dogma of the Catholic Church is defined as a truth revealed by God, which the magisterium (the pope and majority of bishops) of the church declared as binding. There are four approved dogmas related to Mary. The first one is that Mary is the mother of God. This dogma was approved at the Council of Ephesus in 431. Catholics believe Jesus is one divine person with two natures (divine and human). Because this one divine person was born of Mary, then Mary is not just the mother of Jesus but also the mother of God.

The second dogma is that Mary is a perpetual virgin. It was approved in 649. In 1854, the Catholic Church declared Mary was born through an Immaculate Conception, the third dogma. The fourth dogma was approved in 1950, when the church declared Mary's body and soul were taken (assumed) into heaven by Jesus.

It often takes decades, sometimes centuries, for church approval of a new dogma. First, there is a period of much discussion, public statements, and written positions on the subject. Often a conference of ecclesiastical dignitaries and theological experts is assembled to fully investigate the subject and write a position statement. Finally, the pope will ask the bishops from across the world to vote with guidance from the Holy Spirit.

THE IMMACULATE CONCEPTION OF MARY

Catholics believe Mary was born through an Immaculate Conception. That implies she was born without original sin. Catholics believe Mary lived her entire life without sin. The Catholic Church celebrates a liturgical holiday in honor of Mary's Immaculate Conception each year on December 8, which is Mary's birthday.

Catholics also believe Mary was always a virgin—and will always be a virgin. In the original text of the Gospels, the Greek word *adelphos* was used in reference to the brothers of Jesus. However, *adelphos* does not mean blood brothers born of the same parents. The word *adelphos* is used to describe half brothers, stepbrothers, cousins, nephews, or uncles. The Greek word for blood brothers born of the same parents was not used.

The Orthodox Church increasingly speculates Joseph was older than Mary. So he may be a widower who had other children before he married Mary. However, if Mary did have other children, even stepchildren, it is unlikely Jesus would ask John to take care of her following his death on the cross.

THE ASSUMPTION OF MARY'S BODY INTO HEAVEN

Assumption Day is celebrated by Catholics each year on August 15. It's the day they believe Mary's body was taken (assumed) into heaven by Jesus, following the end of her life on earth. It was celebrated universally by the church, beginning in the sixth century. Today it is a holy day of obligation for Catholics in some dioceses, but not all.

The earliest printed reference to Mary's assumption into heaven is in the fourth century, in a document titled "The Falling Asleep of the Holy Mother of God." An apocryphal writing, "The Dormition of the Madonna," also describes Mary being buried in a cave on a stone table before her bodily assumption into heaven.

Tradition places the site of Mary's death at Ephesus and her burial in Jerusalem. Based on historical writings and stories passed down through the ages, it is believed that an angel visited Mary to tell her Jesus would take her to heaven in three days. Three days later, Mary fell asleep in John's house where she resided. The house was in Ephesus on Mount Zion, steps away from the Upper Room where the Last Supper took place. Jesus immediately took her soul to heaven. Mary's body was buried in a cave at the foot of the Mount of Olives in the Kidron Valley of the city of Jerusalem. After three days, Jesus assumed Mary's body into heaven.

The Church of the Dormition, located at the hill of Mount Zion in Ephesus, was built over the place where Mary died in order to protect this holy site. It is owned by the Catholic Church.

The Crusader Church, built during the Middle Ages by

Christian Europeans fighting to gain control of the Holy Land from Muslim rule, was built over the grotto (cave) where Mary's body was buried and assumed into heaven in order to protect that holy site. The grotto church is owned by the Greek and Armenian Orthodox churches.

The Crusader Church is built in the shape of a cross. The chapel of Mary's empty tomb is in the eastern hall. Two sides of the tomb are covered in glass, allowing visitors to see it is empty. There are three holes cut into the back wall, allowing visitors to touch the inside of the empty tomb. The Crusader Church also houses a chapel honoring Mary's parents, Hanna (Anna) and Joachim.

MARY ALWAYS DEFERS TO JESUS

Mary is always deferential to her Son, Jesus. In apparitions, paintings, and statues, she points toward Jesus or heaven. When holding a baby Jesus, her hand gestures toward him. When alone, her hands point toward heaven. Mary always wears clothing in colors representing earth, not divinity. Jesus is often depicted wearing red clothing representative of divinity.

Through the centuries, there have been numerous apparitions of Mary in different parts of the world. These are times when Mary visits her "earthly children" to save nonbelievers and to encourage believers to be stronger in their faith. Often, these visits occur prior to major wars or disease, when many souls may be lost. Mary speaks to the world through messages given to visionaries, who are often children. The Blessed Mother Mary openly weeps for her earthly children who may be lost for eternity in hell.

In the earlier centuries, when Mary visited earth, she often communicated without speaking, through silence. In the Middle Ages, Mary would speak to visionaries using few words. In more modern times, Mary has much to communicate to the world. Through lengthy visits with visionaries spanning decades, Mary openly answers many questions about heaven and hell, other religions, and how Christians should live while on earth. Her ongoing messages in the village of Medjugorje, in the former Yugoslavia, are most informative. Everyone should listen carefully to what she has to say.

PRAYERS TO MARY

"Hail Mary," the famous prayer to Mary for intercession with Jesus, is recited by many Catholics from memory. It is based on Bible verses from the first chapter of the Gospel of Luke (Luke 1:28, 42). The Hail Mary prayer was set to music by Franz Schubert in 1825 and is known as "Ave Maria." It is usually sung in Latin.

PRAYING THE ROSARY

All Christians believe private confession of sins to God allows each sin to be forgiven. Protestants believe confessing their sins directly to God will result in forgiveness. They may voluntarily pay for damages or stolen property following a private confession to God. However, any restitution or making amends for those sins is often forgotten by many and remains unusual. Catholics often confess sins to God through a Catholic priest, which usually results in both forgiveness and making amends.

A common form of restitution recommended by a Catholic priest following confession of sins is to pray the Rosary a specific number of times. Praying the Rosary is a lengthy Catholic prayer using standard prayers based on the Bible. The Rosary begins with the Apostle's Creed, followed by the Lord's Prayer. The standard Catholic prayers of Hail Mary and Glory Be (the Doxology) are recited multiple times. The Lord's Prayer is repeated and followed by additional Hail Mary and Glory Be prayers.

This sequence is repeated a total of six times. Other standard Catholic prayers are included throughout the Holy Rosary prayer. When praying a complete Rosary, the Lord's Prayer is repeated six different times. It may take fifteen to twenty minutes to completely pray the Rosary properly.

A beaded necklace-type rosary is usually held in your hand when praying the Holy Rosary. It consists of fifty-nine beads, a crucifix, and a medal. A crucifix is a cross with a representation of Jesus hanging on the cross. Praying the Rosary begins by making the sign of the cross. Next, the cross on the necklace-type rosary is held between your fingers while saying the Apostle's Creed. Your fingers then move to the first bead on the rosary to pray the Lord's Prayer. Your fingers move from bead to bead along the rosary when praying each prayer or set of prayers. Because of the number of repetitions of prayers, the rosary beads help keep count to ensure the Rosary prayer is properly completed. The Holy Rosary prayer is concluded by making the sign of the cross a second time.

Catholics often share the purpose or intention of their prayer silently to God just prior to praying the Holy Rosary or other common prayers. They believe God understands the intention of their prayer whether the intention is spoken or unspoken and does not need to be included in the prayer itself.

THE SIGN OF THE CROSS

Catholics often make the sign of the cross to profess Christian faith or invoke divine protection or blessing. When touching the forehead with their fingers they say, "In the name of the Father" which represents God the Father. Next, touching the middle of the chest, they say, "And of the Son" which represents Jesus Christ the Son of God. Then touching the left and right shoulder, they say, "And of the Holy Spirit, Amen," which represents the Holy Spirit. The sign of the cross is an outward showing of the Trinity and is said either quietly or silently.

MARY APPEARS IN APPARITIONS

The Catholic Church believes it is possible for men and women to receive supernatural visits known as apparitions. They experience them through actual messages, revelations of the Holy Spirit, Jesus,

Mary, angels, or saints. This physical encounter is intended for either the recipient or their community. The nature of the Catholic religion, focused on private prayer and personal meditation, helps parishioners understand the importance of visible signs. Even though the soul is the preferred channel for dialogue between humans and God, sometimes his presence is manifested on a level more suited to an earthly nature. During supernatural apparitions, God's love becomes visible and transcends understanding.

The Catholic Church views Mary's apparitions as interventions from a loving mother toward her children. They are acts of mercy and love from someone who does not forget those who live the anxieties of earthly life. Mary occasionally appears to men and women to remind believers of her Son's passion and grace.

MARY'S CALL TO PRAYER

Mary calls the faithful to pray more often. After the ascension of Jesus, the Holy Spirit came to give Christians special spiritual powers on earth. With faith in Christ, Christian prayer can result in miracles. This is a powerful gift that is little used in the world today.

Through prayer, illnesses can be cured, wars can be stopped, hearts can be turned, and atheists can be converted to Christ. World leaders can change, and governments opposed to religion can be altered to support religion. More prayers coupled with faith in Christ are urgently needed.

When Christians do not pray adequately, atheism grows. Without sufficient prayer, wars, epidemics, and famines abound. Without prayer and faith in Christ, governments take away religious rights from the faithful. With her call to prayer, Mary reminds Christians to use the power of prayer to reverse these disturbing trends.

CHAPTER 5
THE PROTESTANT VIEW OF MARY

Most Protestants respect Mary as the mother of Jesus but show little devotion to her. They are careful to display all worship and sacred respect only to Jesus and his heavenly Father but not to Mary. Many Protestants believe Mary was a virgin when Jesus was born. However, they take different positions on how long she remained a virgin.

Many Protestant Christians misunderstand the Catholic devotion to Mary. Catholics do not worship Mary, only God. However, they do honor Mary. Catholics believe that honoring Mary can lead Christians to a closer relationship with Jesus. The scriptures, through the Gospel of Luke, explain when Mary is honored, she in turn gives the honor to God.

SOLA SCRIPTURA

The Protestant Reformation occurred in 1517. Martin Luther is often credited with leading the schism in the Christian Church that formed Protestantism and Catholicism. However, Ulrich Zwingli also led a major Protestant break from the church during that time. Both men were educated sufficiently to make their own biblical translations.

Luther implemented the *sola scriptura* concept as he originally designed it. The Bible and church tradition would both help determine church doctrine, not just the Bible. His intention was only that tradition not take priority over the Bible. Lutheranism retained many of the Catholic traditions like honoring the Blessed Virgin Mary and personal participation in confession to a priest. Even though Luther named his new concept "only scripture," he always intended to use church tradition.

Zwingli's view of *sola scriptura* went further than Luther's. Church traditions not explicitly included in the Bible were eliminated. Protestant Anabaptists implemented a more radical version of *sola scriptura,* which resulted in the simplest form of worship possible. Many religious traditions, like honoring Mary and praying to saints, were removed from practice altogether.

FEW BIBLE REFERENCES TO MARY

Catholics base their doctrine on both the Bible and tradition. Tradition includes rituals and practices of Christ's disciples and early church writings. These were passed down from generation to generation for two thousand years. As a result, Catholic doctrine concerning Mary is rich with devotion and honor for her.

Protestants base their doctrinal beliefs primarily on the Bible and not on tradition. During the time of Jesus, when the New Testament was written, women were considered unimportant to Jewish men. So little was written about Mary in the Bible. Without the use of tradition, and with little information in the Bible about Mary, it follows that Protestant doctrine contains very little about Mary. Protestants respect Mary as the mother of Jesus, but they exhibit little devotion or religious honor to her.

MARY DOES NOT CALL CHRISTIANS TO CHANGE DENOMINATIONS

During her apparitions, Mary's call to prayer is for all Christians, whether they are Protestant, Catholic, Orthodox, or Anglican. Mary does not explicitly mention any Protestant denomination, Orthodox Church, or Catholic Church. She refers to all Christians as "the faithful."

PROTESTANT PRAYER MINISTRIES

Prayer for others is very consistent with Protestant prayer ministries. Many Protestants organize women's prayer groups, men's prayer groups, and interdenominational prayer groups. Protestant churches often have healing prayer ministries and mission prayer ministries.

During her visits to earth, Mary's primary concern is the growing number of atheists in the world. She asks all Christians to pray for atheists to convert to Christianity before it is too late. More Christian prayers are needed. Mary's request is very consistent with existing Protestant prayer ministries, a Protestant mission to convert nonbelievers, and a Protestant belief in miracles.

MARY'S APPARITIONS

In each of Mary's apparitions, she appears in brilliant light. Her actions and messages are focused on devotion to her Son, Jesus. Mary shows love and compassion for the people on earth, whom she views as her children. She feels deep sorrow for lost sinners.

Reminiscent of Pentecost, Mary speaks to each visionary in their own language, even when it's a rare dialect. She speaks to them in terms they understand. When speaking to Catholics, she asks them to pray the Rosary. Because Protestants do not use a rosary, they should interpret Mary's message simply as praying more using the type of prayer to which they are accustomed. All Christians can reduce the widespread increase in atheism in the world with more prayers.

Similarly, when Mary says God plans to inflict chastisement on the earth in the form of war or famine, this should not be interpreted literally. Due to insufficient prayer, humanity incurs devastating war and famine. God allows calamities in the world because humans have free will. However, God is often frustrated with Christians because they do not use the wonderful gift of prayer through the Holy Spirit to avoid these calamities.

Mary seems to visit earth when a large group of people are most vulnerable. In some instances, there is an impending war, plague, or famine. Mary comes to save souls and revive the Christian faith in those who have lost their faith. Mary weeps for the nonbelievers who may soon die from war or disease and live in hell for eternity.

At times, Mary asks for a chapel to be built. She often provides a spring of healing water to attract crowds of people for miracle healings. She knows a miracle ministry brings more people closer to God and converts atheists into believers.

At other times, Mary visits earth once a war or plague is past. When a large group of people lose faith following troubled times and great personal loss, Mary comes to show love and compassion. She reminds them of the sacrifice made by her Son on the cross. Mary works to revive Christian faith in the community. She uses a miracle ministry to communicate her Son's message to a larger audience. This often results in more souls saved and restoration of a community's faith.

EIGHTEEN SHORT STORIES

Whether you believe the Catholic view of Mary or the Protestant view of Mary is not important. However, Mary's messages to the world are critical for all Christians to understand. She cares deeply for people. Mary wants all Christians to know how they can use a more active prayer life to save souls.

A single Marian visitation story is summarized in each of the next eighteen chapters. They are arranged chronologically to reveal a clearer perspective of changes in Mary's approach over time. This also allows for a better understanding of changes in Mary's level of urgency across the centuries. Each of the eighteen stories articulates messages from Mary that lead Christians to the Father through her Son, Jesus.

CHAPTER 6
1531: APPARITION IN MEXICO CITY, MEXICO

On December 9, 1531, a humble peasant named Juan Diego was walking to church in the morning hours. Juan Diego was born in Mexico under Aztec rule. He converted to Catholicism and was now fifty-seven years old.

While walking, Juan Diego heard strange music. He later described the music as the beautiful sounds of birds. Juan Diego changed direction to investigate when he suddenly saw an apparition of the Virgin Mary. She was surrounded by a ball of light as bright as the sun. Mary calmed Juan Diego and identified herself as the "Mother of the True God."

Mary and Juan Diego were standing on Tepeyac Hill, the site of a former Aztec temple, just northwest of Mexico City. Mary brought a message of love and compassion for the world. Mary told Juan Diego to ask the bishop to build a church on the site of the apparition.

Juan Diego did as he was instructed. When the bishop refused, Juan Diego reported back to Mary. She told him to ask the bishop again the next morning. Juan Diego met with the bishop again. This time, the bishop requested a sign from Mary before he would agree to build a church. Juan Diego again reported the bishop's response back to Mary.

Mary instructed Juan Diego to take some roses and keep them hidden inside the front of his tilma, an outer garment worn by men, until he met with the bishop for the third time. Juan Diego complied with her instructions. Upon meeting the bishop, Juan Diego opened his tilma and let the roses cascade to the floor. Both men were astonished to see a beautiful painting of Mary on the front of Juan Diego's tilma. The bishop realized it was a sign from Mary and knelt before it. He agreed to construct a church on Tepeyac Hill, as Mary requested.

In the painting, Mary stands just as she first appeared to Juan Diego, a native princess with a mestizo face and high cheekbones. Her head is bowed, and her hands are folded in prayer to God. Under her feet is a crescent moon, a symbol of the Aztec religion. One message from the painting is that she is more powerful than Aztec gods, yet she herself is not God.

MANY SOULS ARE SAVED

Symbolism throughout the painting communicated many messages to the Aztec people. During that time, Aztecs worshipped the sun. Out of fear the world would soon end, they practiced daily human sacrifice of Aztec children to symbolically feed the sun with blood. In the painting, Our Lady of Guadalupe (the name Mary chose) is shining as bright as the sun. Her long hair is a sign of virginity. She is pregnant with a divine Son who was also sacrificed, giving up his body and blood to pay the price for all humanity. Mary shows a deep love for all people and an understanding that there is no need for any further human sacrifice. Within six years of the apparition, six million Aztecs converted to Christianity.

OUR LADY OF GUADALUPE

Today, the Basilica of Our Lady of Guadalupe houses the original tilma and image of Our Lady of Guadalupe. The garment and painting would normally deteriorate within twenty years. But now, 470 years later, scientists verified both the tilma and the image show no sign of decay. A magnification of Mary's eyes in the painting shows a reflection of what was in front of her in 1531.

In 1921, new government leaders in Mexico plotted to destroy the Catholic Church. Their first target was Our Lady of Guadalupe. A bomb with dynamite was hidden in a basket of flowers and placed at the base of the tilma with the painting of Our Lady of Guadalupe inside the church. The explosion cracked some of the marble in the church. Windows in houses outside of the church were blown out. However, the painting and tilma were undamaged. Even its glass cover remained unbroken.

CONCLUDING EVENTS

In 1555, Tepeyac Hill was approved by the Vatican as a Marian apparition site. Twenty-five popes officially honored Our Lady of Guadalupe. Pope John Paul II visited the Basilica of Our Lady of Guadalupe four times. On his third visit, John Paul declared the date of December 12 as a Liturgical Holy Day for the entire continent. In 2000, Pope John Paul II canonized Juan Diego as a saint.

The site is visited by twenty million people each year. Because Mary appeared in this apparition with olive-colored skin, people from across the world with olive-colored skin are especially comforted by Our Lady of Guadalupe. The church is known for many miracles, cures, interventions, and conversions to Christianity.

KEY MESSAGES FROM BLESSED MARY

Mary's motherly love and compassion for the Aztec people of Mexico result in more than six million conversions to Christianity within six years of the apparition. The number of saved Christians multiply with future generations. As the result of a story told through a divine picture, Aztecs understand they do not need to sacrifice their children. The sacrifice of Mary's Son, Jesus, was sufficient for all humanity.

God performs miracles of healing at this site in Mexico City. God continues to save souls by conversion to Christianity once they personally understand the story of Mary's visit here.

CHAPTER 7
1594: Apparition in Quito, Ecuador

In 1566, Mariana de Jesus Torres, at the young age of thirteen, left her homeland in Spain with her aunt to establish a Conceptionist order of nuns in Quito, Ecuador. Mariana's aunt was the cousin of Spain's King Philip II. At the time, Ecuador was under Spanish rule and remained that way until the nineteenth century.

Sister Mariana experienced seven Marian apparitions over a forty-year period, from February 2, 1594, until February 2, 1634. During the apparitions, Mary made many predictions about Ecuador and the world, and all have come true except one. The final prediction concerns the world near the late stages of the twentieth century and is not fully complete.

On the voyage from Spain to Ecuador, a great storm arose. Satan, in the form of a seven-headed serpent, ascended from the sea to stop the women and their mission. Blessed Mary appeared with the Christ child, holding a cross with a lance at the end of it. She slew the serpent, and the storm cleared. To this day, the convent sisters in Quito wear a badge to commemorate this event.

DEATH AND RESURRECTION

In 1582, at age nineteen, Mariana saw a vision of the tabernacle door open and Christ emerge from his sufferings at Calvary while Christ's mother cried. Mariana asked if she was to blame. Mary replied, "No, not you, but the criminal world of the twentieth century." Then Mariana saw three swords over the head of Christ, which represented punishment for the twentieth century and beyond. Words written on the swords were: "I will punish heresy," "I will punish blasphemy," and "I will punish impurity."

When Mary asked Mariana to suffer for the sins of the twentieth century, she agreed. The swords fell from Christ's head and plunged into Mariana. She died and appeared at the judgment seat of Christ. After she was judged blameless, she chose to return to earth and suffer for the sins of the twentieth century instead of immediately going to heaven. Mariana was miraculously resurrected.

To very holy Catholics, suffering is like a spiritual currency. It is a way for Christians to participate in the suffering of Christ. Through prayer, personal suffering can be offered as spiritual currency to help others in need.

A NEW STATUE

During an apparition in 1610, the Blessed Mother asked Sister Mariana to have a specific statue of Mary made. It should look just as she appeared to Mariana, except Mary should hold the infant Jesus in her left arm and a staff and keys in her right hand. The presence of the divine infant was to remind everyone how powerful Mary is in bringing people to her Son: "To Jesus, through Mary." The keys and staff symbolize Mary's role as the true and perpetual abbess to the convent. (She explained that the Lord desired this statue be made for two reasons: first, for the people of the city of Quito and the whole world so they might have recourse to her in the difficult days ahead; second, so that throughout time, her daughters in the convent should come to her as their mother and abbess.) Therefore, her staff points outward, indicating an authority extending beyond the walls of the convent.

On December 8, 1634, archangels Gabriel, Michael, and Raphael appeared to Mariana with Mary. The archangels finished making the statue just as Mary wanted. The statue stands five feet, nine inches tall. It normally resides above the abbess's chair in the upper choir loft of the convent church. During the months of May and October and during the yearly novena (praying for nine days consecutively), the statue is displayed above the high altar.

Few people outside of Ecuador were aware of the statue of Our Lady of the Good Event. It was part of the Blessed Mother's plan to purposely keep it hidden until the last half of the twentieth century. Our Lady of the Good Event is also known as Our Lady of Good Success, due to a language interpretation error.

MARY'S PREDICTION FOR THE VATICAN

On December 8, 1634, during one of Mariana's apparitions, Mary predicted events two hundred years in the future. She said a future Catholic pope would declare the Blessed Mother's Immaculate Conception and pontifical infallibility as two separate dogmas of the church. The same pope would lose control of Rome and the Papal States, to become a prisoner in the Vatican. From 1854 to 1870, all these events came to pass under Pope Pius IX.

MARY'S PREDICTION FOR ECUADOR

Mary also made a prediction for Ecuador in the nineteenth century:

> There will be a truly Catholic president, a man of character to whom God our Lord will give the palm of martyrdom on the square adjoining this convent. While in office, he will consecrate Ecuador to the sacred heart of my most holy son, and this consecration will sustain the Catholic religion in the

> years that will follow, which will be ill-fated ones for the church.

Mary spoke of Gabriel Garcia Moreno, and President Moreno consecrated Ecuador to the Sacred Heart of Jesus in 1873. On August 6, 1875, he was assassinated at Independence Square in Quito, next to the convent.

MARY'S PREDICTION FOR THE TWENTIETH CENTURY

In 1610, Mary predicted a worldwide crisis of faith and morals in the church and society that would begin in the nineteenth century and extend throughout the twentieth century, four hundred years in the future. A "spiritual catastrophe" would begin "shortly after the middle of the twentieth century," which includes the following:

- widespread moral corruption
- contempt for the sacrament of holy matrimony
- depraved priests who will scandalize the faithful and cause suffering for good priests
- unbridled lust that will ensnare many souls
- loss of innocence among children and loss of modesty among women
- lack of priestly and religious vocations

Modernism in the church beginning in the late nineteenth century would lead to catastrophe in the late twentieth century.

Mary said all seven of the church sacraments would come under attack:

> It will be difficult to receive the Sacrament of Baptism and also that of Confirmation … the devil will make a great effort to destroy the Sacrament

> of Confession by means of people in positions of authority.

The Holy Eucharist will be defiled:

> The enemies of Jesus Christ, instigated by the devil, will steal consecrated hosts from the churches so that they may profane the Eucharistic species. My most holy son will see himself cast upon the ground and trampled upon by filthy feet.

The Catholic Church believes the Eucharist or host, which is Communion bread, becomes the body of Christ when consecrated by a priest.

People will disrespect the Sacrament of Holy Unction, commonly called "Last Rites," and many will die without receiving it. Because of this, Mary says, "many souls will be deprived of innumerable graces, consolations, and the strength they need to make that great leap from time to eternity."

The Sacrament of Holy Matrimony will be defiled in:

> iniquitous laws with the objective of doing away with this Sacrament, making it easy for everyone to live in sin, encouraging the procreation of illegitimate children born without the blessing of the church. The Christian spirit will rapidly decay, extinguishing the precious light of faith until it reaches a point that there will be an almost total and general corruption of customs.

Those in the priesthood and other religious vocations will lessen:

> The Sacrament of Holy Orders will be ridiculed, oppressed, and despised … the demon will try to

> persecute ministers of the Lord in every possible way and he will labor with cruel and subtle astuteness to deviate them from the spirit of their vocation, corrupting many of them.

Mary also spoke of the value of convents and monasteries. She said people on earth do not understand the power of prayer. Prayers from monasteries and convents result in the salvation of souls, the conversion of great sinners, the deferral of plagues, the production and fertility of land, the end of wars, and harmony among nations.

Along with this dark prediction for our times, Mary also offers a resolution to the crisis. Mary says devotion to her, which she then gives to Jesus, under Our Lady of the Good Event, will result in triumph. The mother of God promises that just when it seems all is lost, she will intervene and initiate:

> the happy beginning of the complete restoration. This will mark the arrival of my hour, when I, in a marvelous way, will dethrone the proud and cursed Satan, trampling him under my feet and fettering him in the infernal abyss.

CHASTISEMENT FOR THE WORLD

Due to the corruption and many sins of the world, there will be a period of chastisement for the world in the middle to late twentieth century. In an extraordinary vision, Christ shared his feelings with Mariana.

Mariana explained that the ingratitude and betrayal of religious souls, so dear to Jesus's heart, would compel the Lord to let justice fall upon his beloved monasteries, convents, and cathedrals, even over entire cities. When those so near to him, who belong to him, reject his Spirit and abandon him alone in tabernacles, rarely remembering that he lives there especially for love of them, chastisement will come. (In the Catholic Church, a tabernacle is an ornate box that holds consecrated Communion hosts.)

Imprudent admissions and internal abuses permitted by superiors are the ruin of religious communities. Such communities can only be preserved at the cost of much penance, humiliation, and daily practice of religious virtues by those religious who are good. Woe to those corrupt members during the times of calamity! Weep for them and implore that the time of so much suffering will be shortened.

Mariana warned that the chastisement would be severe for those religious who squandered so many graces with their pride and vainglory to secure positions of power and rank. The lukewarm religious leaders are especially condemned. If men, and above all, priests, and religious souls, would only realize how greatly Jesus is wounded and displeased with the coldness, indifference, and lack of confidence on the part of those who so closely belong to him. He will not tolerate this. Halfway measures are not pleasing to him. He desires all or nothing. According to his example, Jesus gave himself to the last drop of blood from his shattered body on the cross. However, he continued to live in the tabernacle under the same roof with these hidden souls, exposing himself to so many profanations and sacrileges. Jesus knows well all that takes place there.

SISTER MARIANA

The apparitions of Blessed Mary to Sister Mariana were approved by a Catholic bishop in 1611. Sister Mariana was named "Servant of God." The process of her canonization to saint is ongoing. The convent church was named an archdiocesan Marian sanctuary in 1991, making it an official place of pilgrimage.

Sister Mariana died in 1635. When her casket was opened in 1906, her body was found to show no decomposition. There was no odor from her body other than the fragrance of lilies. The Catholic Church refers to this phenomenon as an incorruptible body.

There are dozens of Catholic saints determined by the Vatican to have incorruptible bodies. They are in Italy, France, and throughout the world. Some are on display in glass coffins, interred under church altars, buried underground, or placed in church basement crypts.

KEY MESSAGES FROM BLESSED MARY

Mary correctly predicts future events that occur centuries later. In the 1600s, Mary predicts events affecting the Vatican, Ecuador, and the twentieth century. Most concerning to Mary is a "spiritual catastrophe" that occurs in the late twentieth century. The spiritual catastrophe incudes widespread moral corruption in the church, unbridled lust and contempt for holy matrimony, loss of innocence among children, and a shortage of priests.

Mary cautions the faithful about corruption in the church. She encourages the faithful to pray and grow closer to God.

We still await Mary's promise to intervene and initiate the happy beginning of the complete restoration, when she will dethrone the proud and cursed Satan.

CHAPTER 8
1830: APPARITION IN PARIS, FRANCE

Catherine Laboure was born in Burgundy, France, as the ninth of eleven children. From an early age, Catherine felt a call to religious life. When she was nine years old, Catherine's mother died. After the funeral, Catherine retreated to her room, stood on a chair to reach a statue of Mary, and kissed it. She told Mary, "Now you will be my mother."

Catherine's father gave her the responsibility of caring for the household. She dutifully and lovingly did as she was asked. Three years later, Catherine made her First Communion.

BECOMING A NUN

One day, she had a dream in which an older priest motioned her to a roomful of sick people. He said, "It is a good deed to look after the sick. God has designs on you. Do not forget it."

Years later, Catherine visited a hospital of the Daughters of Charity and noticed a picture of the same priest from her dream on the wall. When she asked about him, she was told the priest was their founder, St. Vincent de Paul. Catherine immediately knew she would become a member of St. Vincent's order.

In January of 1830, Catherine Laboure became a nun in the

Daughters of Charity. Three months later, she traveled to Paris and entered the Mother House of the order. On July 19, 1830, after hearing a homily about St. Vincent de Paul, twenty-four-year-old Catherine prayed to the saint and requested to see the mother of God with her own eyes. That same night, a bright light awoke her. Her guardian angel instructed her to follow him to the chapel, where the Virgin Mary was waiting for her.

Catherine opened the door to the chapel and saw a brilliant light. She went up to the communion rail and knelt prayerfully. After hearing the swishing sound of a silk gown, she turned and saw Blessed Mary seated in the priest's chair. Catherine quickly found herself on her knees in front of the Blessed Virgin, with her hands prayerfully folded on Mary's knees. It was the beginning of a two-hour conversation.

Mary told her that God will give her a mission:

> You will have the protection of God and St. Vincent. I always will have my eyes upon you. There will be much persecution. The cross will be treated with contempt. It will be hurled to the ground and blood will flow. The side of our Lord will be pierced again.

Mary appeared sorrowful but encouraging. She said, "But come to the foot of this altar and here graces will be bestowed upon all who ask with confidence and fervor. They will be given to the rich and poor." Then Mary faded away.

Four months later, on November 27, 1830, Catherine and the other sisters were in the chapel for evening prayers and meditation. Catherine heard the swishing sound of a silk gown and turned. It was the Blessed Virgin Mary appearing to the left of the painting of St. Joseph.

This apparition was conducted entirely without speaking. Mary was dressed in white silk, standing on a white globe, and holding a golden ball adorned with a cross. There were three rings on each of her fingers. Each ring had gemstones. The larger gemstones were emitting rays of flashing light.

> This ball which you see is the world; I am praying for it and for everyone in the world. The rays are the graces which I give to everyone who asks for them. But there are no rays for some of these stones; many people do not receive graces because they do not ask for them.

VISION OF THE MIRACULOUS MEDAL

Then the apparition quickly changed. Mary had her arms outstretched inside an oval frame with golden lettering and the words: "O Mary conceived without sin, pray for us who have recourse to thee." Mary was standing on a globe, as queen of heaven and earth, while crushing the head of a green serpent under her foot. Mary gave the following instruction:

> Have a medal struck on this model. All those who carry this will receive grace in abundance, especially if they wear the medal around their neck and say this prayer confidently. They will receive special protection from the mother of God and abundant graces.

Then the whole scene turned around, and Catherine could see the back of the medal. A letter "M" was in the center. A cross ascended, and its base passed through the "M." Below were the two hearts of Jesus and Mary, one crowned with thorns and the other pierced by the sword of sorrow. The whole scene was surrounded by a crown of twelve stars.

Mary said, "The M with the cross and the two hearts say enough."

During the following year, this apparition occurred five times, and each time it came with the same instructions: "Have a medal struck on this model, and all those who wear it will receive great graces, especially when worn around the neck."

Catherine endured much humiliation. It took two years before her young confessor priest believed her. The priest finally went to the archbishop and requested the medals. The archbishop ordered 1,500 medals to be struck.

In February 1832, Paris was devastated by a cholera epidemic that caused twenty thousand deaths. The Daughters of Charity distributed two thousand medals in the Paris area. Miraculous healings occurred quickly, and conversions followed. Parisians started to call the medals "miraculous."

Beyond the cholera epidemic in Paris, those who wore the medal received many answered prayers, conversions, miracle healings, bad habits broken, dangers averted, and blessings bestowed. Recorded cures included those with insanity, tuberculosis, epilepsy, paralysis, fractures, and fevers.

In a written record from Catherine's confessor priest, miraculous conversions due to Mary's intercession through the Miraculous Medal included hardened sinners, atheists, evildoers, and lukewarm souls.

CONCLUDING EVENTS

More than ten million medals were sold during the first five years. At the time of Catherine's death, more than one billion Miraculous Medals had been made. In Philadelphia, 750,000 graces were granted and recorded between 1930 and 1950. A Miraculous Medal Shrine was constructed in Philadelphia.

The original name of the medal was "Medal of the Immaculate Conception." However, after seven years, the public began calling it the "Miraculous Medal" because of the many miracles. The apparitions were authenticated by the Vatican in 1836.

Catherine sought no attention for the medals. Over the next

forty years, she quietly cared for the elderly, infirm, and disabled. On New Year's Eve, 1876, at age seventy, Sister Catherine passed away. Only a few people around her knew she was the one who received the Miraculous Medal from the Blessed Virgin Mary.

The Miraculous Medal is a symbol of devotion and faith, of the endless grace the Virgin Mary gives to her children on earth. It is a support for those needing grace, for those facing turbulent times, and for those who need to remember they are not alone. Mary will support and sustain them as a good and loving mother.

The nature of the Catholic religion is deeply focused on a personal relationship with God through prayer and meditation. A veneration object with powerful symbolism, given through a heavenly apparition and capable of channeling unexpected healings, brings untold blessings to those who believe.

More than fifty years after her death, Catherine's body was exhumed in 1933. Miraculously, her body was incorrupt, meaning it was not in a decayed state, but as fresh as the day she was buried. Her body can still be seen at the Daughters of Charity on Rue du Bac 140 in Paris, France.

Catherine was canonized as a saint on July 27, 1947, by Pope Pius XII. Many believers in Christ attended the ceremony. The audience included ten thousand people who wore their Miraculous Medals.

KEY MESSAGES FROM BLESSED MARY

Showing motherly love and compassion for all people, Mary comes to give graces to the faithful. Whether rich or poor, graces are available to those who ask with confidence and fervor. Mary came to intercede with her Son, Jesus, asking him to perform healing miracles and grant other graces to those with faith in him. Mary comes to encourage the faithful to seek Christ and to convert souls to Christ once they hear and understand God's power through miracles.

CHAPTER 9

1842: Apparition in Rome, Italy

Ten years after the introduction of the Miraculous Medal, Mary returned to earth in response to someone using the medal. A convert to Catholicism incessantly proselytized to others. On one occasion, he gifted a Miraculous Medal to a friend and prayed for their conversion with fervor.

Marie "Alphonse" Ratisbonne and his brother, Theodor, were born into a wealthy Jewish family of bankers in Strasbourg, France. When Alphonse was still a child, Theodor converted to Catholicism and became a priest. The family reacted with hostility, and Alphonse promised never to speak to his brother again. Alphonse developed a total disdain for Catholicism and ignored God altogether.

In 1842, at age twenty-eight, Alphonse became engaged to marry. Before the wedding, he planned to first tour Europe. From Naples, Alphonse mistakenly boarded the wrong train and went to Rome instead of Palermo. While touring Rome, he met an old classmate from Strasbourg, Gustave de Bussieres, a Protestant. They rekindled their friendship.

Alphonse later went to visit Gustave in Rome and met Gustave's older brother, Baron Theodore de Bussieres. Theodore was a convert to Catholicism and a close friend of Alphonse's older priest brother.

Although they disagreed about Catholicism, Alphonse and the baron became friends.

RELENTLESS PROSELYTISM

The baron challenged Alphonse to wear a Catholic medal around his neck, the Miraculous Medal, and to recite the Memorare, a short Catholic prayer, every morning and evening. Alphonse did not want to appear petty and accepted the challenge. However, Alphonse began to lose patience with the baron's relentless proselytism.

The baron prayed for the conversion of Alphonse. He also asked his many friends to pray extra Memorares for his conversion. The baron asked Alphonse to meet him a few days later in the Basilica of St. Andrea delle Fratte on January 20, 1842.

When the baron saw Alphonse in the basilica, Alphonse said,

> I was scarcely in the church when total confusion came over me. When I looked up, it seemed to me that the entire church had been swallowed up in shadow, except one chapel. It was as though all the light was concentrated in that single space. I looked over toward this chapel whence so much light shone, and above the altar was a living figure, tall, majestic, beautiful, and full of mercy. It was the most holy Virgin Mary, resembling her figure on the Miraculous Medal. At this sight, I fell on my knees right where I stood. Unable to look up because of the blinding light, I fixed my glance on her hands, and in them I could read the expression of mercy and pardon. In the presence of the most blessed virgin, even though she did not speak a word to me, I understood the frightful situation I was in, my sins and the beauty of the Catholic faith.

Alphonse was sobbing when the baron helped him to a carriage and brought him to the hotel where he was staying. Alphonse entered the convent of the Jesuits and received baptism, confirmation, and his first Holy Communion.

CONCLUDING EVENTS

In May of 1842, a few months after the apparition, a painting of Mary was placed in the basilica where she appeared. Natale Carta painted it according to Alphonse's description of how Mary looked. On June 3, 1942, after investigation by Catholic authorities, the bishop approved the conversion of Alphonse as an authentic miracle, implying the apparition of Mary was also approved.

In 1847, Alphonse was ordained as a priest and entered the Society of Jesus to devote himself to the conversion of Jews. With permission from Pope Pius IX, Alphonse left the society and relocated to Jerusalem. There he built a large convent and school with an orphanage for girls. Nearby, he erected a second convent with a church and another orphanage for girls. Alphonse labored for the conversion of Jews and Muslims until his death in 1884.

On January 17, 1892, Pope Leo XIII added a royal diadem (crown) to Mary's painting because there were so many miracles performed in the basilica's chapel through Mary's intercession. In 1942, the church was elevated to the rank of basilica. In 1960, it was elevated to a cardinal's church. Pope John Paul II visited this church on February 28, 1982.

KEY MESSAGES FROM BLESSED MARY

Mary comes to convert souls to Christ. With the miracle of her apparition, one man converts to Christianity and goes on to convert many other souls to Christ. God performs miracles of healing and conversion at the site of the apparition.

In a twentieth-century apparition, Mary further clarifies that her Son, Jesus, accepts other religions like Judaism and Islam. However, the person still needs to have faith in God to be rewarded with heaven.

CHAPTER 10
1846: Apparition in La Salette, France

Life in France was exceedingly difficult in 1846. It would become worse before it began to improve. France was going through both a financial crisis and a bleak harvest. There was an increasing secularization of thought among the population. Fewer people were attending Mass, and the sacraments were neglected. Prayers were forgotten. An economic depression hit the country in 1847. Peasant groups attempted rebellions, but they were crushed each time.

The French Revolution of 1848 overthrew the monarchy of King Louis Philippe and created the conservative French Second Republic. Only a few months later, a bloody rebellion to overthrow the new republic by Paris workers was unsuccessful. In December 1848, Louis Napoleon Bonaparte (Napoleon III) was elected president of the French Second Republic. Napoleon III led France in wars with Prussia, Italy, and other countries.

THE APPARITIONS

Knowing many lives could be lost during current and future difficulties, Mary visited earth to convert souls and call for prayer, while there was still time. On Saturday afternoon, September 19,

1846, two children, eleven-year-old Maximin Guiraud and fourteen-year-old Melanie Calvat, were tending sheep in a high pasture in the Alps above the village of La Salette, France. Both children were from poor families. They had no schooling and rarely attended Mass.

When the two children looked up, they saw a brilliant light, brighter than the sun. They could see a beautiful lady seated on a rock. She was crying. The lady's clothes were white, with a white shawl, and appeared like beams of light. She had a large crucifix hanging from her neck, with a brilliant figure of Christ on it. Her slippers were edged with roses. On her head was a lucent crown with a band of roses.

The lady said, "Come to me, my children. Do not be afraid. I am here to tell something of greatest importance. If my people will not obey, I shall be compelled to loosen my Son's arm. It is so heavy, so pressing, that I can no longer restrain it. How long I have suffered for you! If my Son is not to cast you off, I am obliged to entreat him without ceasing. But you take not the least notice of that. No matter how well you pray in the future, no matter how well you act, you will never be able to make up to me what I have endured for your sake.

"I have appointed you six days for working. The seventh I have reserved for myself. And no one will give it to me. This is what causes the weight of my Son's arm to be crushing. The cart drivers cannot swear without bringing in my Son's name. These are the two things that make my Son's arms so burdensome.

"If the harvest is spoiled, it is your own fault. I warned you last year by means of the potatoes. You paid no heed. Quite the reverse, when you discovered that the potatoes had rotted, you swore, you abused my Son's name. They will continue to rot, and by Christmas this year, there will be none left.

"If you have grain, it will do no good to sow it, for what you sow, the beasts will devour, and any part of it that springs up will crumble into dust when you thresh it. A great famine is coming. But before that happens, the children under seven years of age will be seized with trembling and die in their parents' arms. The grown-ups will pay for their sins by hunger. The grapes will rot, and the walnuts will turn bad.

"If people are converted, the rocks will become piles of wheat, and it will be found that the potatoes have sown themselves." She asked if the children said their prayers.

They replied, "Hardly at all."

The lady said, "Ah, my children, it is especially important to say them, at night and in the morning. When you do not have time, at least say an Our Father and a Hail Mary. And when you can, say more.

"Only a few rather old women go to Mass in the summer. All the rest work every Sunday throughout the summer. And in winter, when they don't know what to do with themselves, they go to Mass only to poke fun at religion. During Lent, they flock to the butcher shops, like dogs. My children, you will make this known to all my people." Then the lady walked up a path and disappeared in a bright light.

The children told their employers, families, and friends. They were sent to the local parish priest, and he repeated their story during Mass. Government officials investigated. Despite threats of imprisonment, each child repeated the identical story.

Someone went to the apparition site and broke off a piece of the rock where Mary sat. A spring of water emerged where it was usually dry. The spring flowed abundantly. Some spring water was given to a woman with a serious illness. She drank the water each day as she prayed a novena. On the ninth day, she was healed.

Other healing miracles occurred there. People began to attend Mass each Sunday. They stopped working on Sundays and prayed faithfully. Pilgrimages to the site became more popular.

OUR LADY OF LA SALETTE

Five years after the apparition, on September 19, 1851, the Vatican determined the apparition to be authentic. A cornerstone to a new basilica was laid in honor of Our Lady of La Salette. A new religious community, the Missionaries of La Salette, was formed one year later and presently serve to spread the message of Our Lady of La Salette in twenty-five countries.

KEY MESSAGES FROM BLESSED MARY

During a time of famine, financial crisis, and loss of faith, Mary arrives out of motherly love and compassion. She reminds the people that those who are faithful to God can pray to God for help in their misfortunes. She encourages daily prayer, reserving one day each week for God, regular church attendance, and not taking the Lord's name in vain. Mary starts a revival of Christian faith in the community to save souls. God performs miracles for those with faith in Christ.

CHAPTER 11
1858 APPARITION IN LOURDES, FRANCE

Like many of the peasants who lived in Lourdes, Bernadette Soubirous was born into poverty. Her mother, Louise, married a mill operator at age sixteen. Francois Soubirous was thirty-five years old. When Louise's father died in an accident, the only way to keep the family mill was for one of the owner's daughters to marry the mill operator. Francois Soubirous spurned the custom of marrying the eldest daughter, Bernarde, and married Louise instead.

In January 1844, Bernadette was the first of nine children born to Louise and Francois Soubirous. She was named in honor of her aunt and godmother, Bernarde. Due to disease, five of the nine children died by the age of ten. In 1854, the Soubirous family lost the mill and moved to the slums.

Bernadette had a spleen disorder, stomach problems, and asthma from a bout with cholera. She became a servant girl in a neighboring town to help a large family with their young children, housework, and sheep. Bernadette never complained. She learned how to pray the Holy Rosary on her "two-cent" rosary chain.

On February 11, 1858, at age fourteen, near Lourdes, France, Bernadette heard a gust of wind even though the air was calm. Bernadette was collecting firewood with two companions near the Gave River when she noticed a bright light coming from a cave, or grotto, near the riverbank. She watched as a lady of great beauty emerged from the grotto wearing a pure white robe with a blue sash. She had a rosary on her right arm and yellow roses at her feet. She appeared more brilliant than the sun. The lady smiled peacefully and asked Bernadette to say her Rosary. When Bernadette finished her prayers, the lady had vanished.

A Catholic Mass at the Lourdes grotto.

A statue of Mary in the grotto.

Bernadette felt compelled to return to the grotto and went with friends on February 14. However, only Bernadette could see the apparition. During the apparition, Bernadette's friends tried to move her, but her body could not be budged. Bernadette was in a trancelike state and was unaware of events around her. She could only see and hear the beautiful lady.

Bernadette's parents were upset about the apparition and did not believe her explanation. She was forbidden to return to the grotto. Bernadette's friends made fun of her. Her teacher shook her arm and called her a clown.

Bernadette felt compelled to see the lady again. During her third visit, on February 18, the lady spoke to her. Because Bernadette could only speak a dialect, not the French language, the lady spoke to her using Bernadette's dialect. Her voice was delicate and soft. When the lady asked Bernadette to return to the grotto fifteen more times, she agreed. The lady told Bernadette that although she could not promise her happiness in this world, she did promise happiness would be waiting in heaven.

Thirty people watched Bernadette in the ecstasy of pure joy during the fifth apparition. Some were relatives, and others were people from the village.

After the sixth apparition, Bernadette was ordered to see the priest. He asked many questions, and Bernadette answered them honestly. Bernadette was ordered to the commissioner's office, and she was interrogated. The townspeople started a rumor that Bernadette had seen the Blessed Virgin. The story even appeared in the newspaper. When the commissioner asked Bernadette to confirm it was the Blessed Virgin, Bernadette said she was not sure. The lady never told her who she was. The commissioner became enraged and threatened to place Bernadette in prison.

The seventh apparition occurred on February 23. A group of men from the village attended. A doctor, a lawyer, and an army officer watched Bernadette in ecstasy. One of the men held a lighted candle to Bernadette's hand. She never noticed, and it left no burn marks.

During the ninth apparition on February 25, three hundred people gathered at the grotto. Even though they could not see the lady, the crowd watched as Bernadette followed each of Mary's instructions. In compliance with one of Mary's requests, Bernadette entered the left side of the grotto and scraped away the soil. A small trickle of water began to flow from the ground. That afternoon, a few visitors bottled some of the water to drink. Those who drank it felt happy and at peace.

The next day, Bernadette was interrogated by the prosecutor. Like the commissioner, the prosecutor became upset with Bernadette's answers and threatened to put her in prison. She was ordered not to go to the grotto. Bernadette still went because she had made a promise to the lady to return fifteen times.

The thirteenth apparition was on March 2, 1858, with 1,600 people in attendance. The lady told Bernadette to ask the priests to come to the grotto in procession. She also told Bernadette to ask the priests to build a small chapel there so people would visit to worship and gain better access to the healing spring water. She reminded Bernadette to continue to pray for the conversion of sinners.

Bernadette told the priests what the lady asked. The priests bristled at holding a public procession because Bernadette could not even identify the lady. The priests also refused to build a chapel.

The lady eventually revealed herself as "Mary, the mother of Jesus." She also referred to herself as the "Immaculate Conception." Mary shared three secrets with Bernadette, but Bernadette never revealed them. The eighteenth and final apparition occurred on July 16, 1858.

A SPRING OF HOLY WATER

The trickle of water from the ground in the grotto became a spring. Currently, that spring provides twenty-seven thousand gallons of water every day. The grotto at Lourdes quickly became a sacred site for worship. Believers use holy water from the Lourdes spring to perform miracles of healing.

In 1864, the Catholic Church built a statue of Mary in the grotto, using the shape and colors as described by Bernadette. In 1870, church officials built a parish on top of the rock shelf high above the grotto at Lourdes. A three-story basilica, which holds four thousand people, was added in front of the parish in 1889. An additional underground basilica, which holds twenty thousand people, was constructed across the plaza from the first basilica in 1958. Priests hold daily processions on the plaza. Although it was a little late, the Catholic Church met and exceeded the Virgin Mary's request for a procession and a small chapel.

A statue of Mary as she appeared in Lourdes.

Every year, more than five million people from around the world visit the Lourdes shrine in the foothills of the Pyrenees Mountains. The town of Lourdes has a population of fifteen thousand. In all of France, Paris is the only city with more hotels than Lourdes.

At age twenty-two, Bernadette became a nun in the order of the Sisters of Charity and devoted her life to praying for the conversion of sinners. She remained sickly throughout her life, but she never returned to Lourdes to bathe in the healing waters. Bernadette died at age thirty-six and was buried on the convent grounds in Nevers, France.

Her body was exhumed thirty years later, in the presence of two doctors and church leaders. One of the doctors selected by the Catholic Church to examine her body was an atheist pathologist. Church leaders purposely selected a known atheist so the examination results would be believed.

The examination showed no decomposition of the body. There was no odor from her body other than the smell of roses. Her clothing was rotted. The metal in the rosary she was holding had failed, but her body was completely untouched by the laws of nature. The Catholic Church refers to this phenomenon as an incorruptible body. Shortly after this exhumation, the atheist pathologist converted to Catholicism.

A VISIT TO LOURDES

God's presence can be felt at Lourdes from the moment you walk through the entrance gate until the moment you leave. Every day in Lourdes, there are many sick people sitting in wheelchairs and lying on gurneys, all wanting to feel closer to God. Volunteers help move them to various services. Most of the sick stop by the public faucets to gather some holy water from Mary's spring. There are baths available, which also use holy water from the spring.

People in wheelchairs at Lourdes.

Masses in different languages are held throughout each day. Some are outdoor at the grotto where the apparition occurred, and others are held in three different churches on the property. A parish priest from anywhere in the world can reserve a time to hold Mass in his native language for a group of parishioners from his home parish while on a pilgrimage to Lourdes.

Every evening, there is an outdoor Rosary processional with thousands of people who walk in a long line behind volunteers carrying a statue of Mary. Each person in the procession holds a candle. One candle is lit in the front of the processional, and the fire is shared to light everyone's candles as it moves from the front of the processional to the back. As they walk, the crowd recites the Holy Rosary in unison. The service is led by a priest over a loudspeaker. Together, the crowd sings "Ave, Ave, Ave Maria," a popular Catholic hymn, each in their own language except for the chorus, which everyone sings in Latin. The hymn, also known as the "Lourdes Hymn," was written by Jean Gaignet in 1873.

The front of the candlelight processional.

A candlelight processional at Lourdes.

One day each week, an outdoor procession leads into the large, underground basilica for an adoration service. A bishop usually leads this procession while holding a monstrance above his head. The monstrance holds a large Communion wafer, or Eucharist, which becomes the body of Christ when consecrated by a priest. The adoration service is held solely to show adoration for Christ, while in Christ's presence, in the form of the Eucharist.

Across the side street, on the left side of the three-story basilica, a dirt pathway winds up and around a small mountain. Along the path are life-sized stations of the cross, a series of fourteen illustrations representing the successive incidents during the progress of Jesus from his condemnation by Pontius Pilate to his Crucifixion and burial. At the station where Christ hangs on the cross, there are stairs made of wood planks in the dirt. You must go up two flights to reach the Crucifixion station. A sign at the base of the stairs states only people walking up the steps on their knees are sufficiently worthy to visit the Crucifixion scene.

OUR LADY OF LOURDES

Of the five million people who visit Lourdes in southwest France every year, at least half a million are sick and hope to be cured miraculously. There are two hospitals on the complex to care for (but not treat) the sick. The number of miraculous healings at Lourdes is substantial but unknown. There were seven thousand cases of healing reported to the Vatican to request official confirmation as miraculous. So far, after completing thorough investigations, the Catholic Church has officially recognized seventy cases as miraculous. Vatican investigations of the remaining miracle reports are ongoing. Following a theological and medical evaluation, the Lourdes apparition was authenticated by the Vatican on January 18, 1862.

KEY MESSAGES FROM BLESSED MARY

Mary goes to Lourdes to save souls and start a revival of the Christian faith. With water from an underground spring and faith in Christ, God performs many healing miracles. People from all over the world visit Lourdes to experience the feeling of God's presence.

CHAPTER 12

1871: Apparition in Pontmain, France

In 1861, Kaiser Wilhelm I became king of Prussia. He immediately appointed Otto von Bismarck as chancellor. Their goal was to unite all German-speaking states into a single country, even if it meant war. Prussia waged three quick wars in succession. They fought Denmark in 1864 to take over Holstein. Then, in 1866, they fought Austria to combine North and Central Germany under their rule. Finally, Prussia went to war with France in the Franco-Prussian War on August 1, 1870. The superior Prussian army quickly defeated much of the French army. Prussia invaded Paris on December 27 and turned toward Normandy and Brittany in central and northwestern France.

By the middle of January 1871, the Prussian army advanced on Normandy and was just a few miles from the village of Pontmain, France. The Pontmain citizens feared for their lives. The Pontmain parish priest, Father Guerin, instructed the children to pray to the Blessed Mother Mary to intercede with Jesus for protection.

THE APPARITION

On the evening of Tuesday, January 17, 1871, at about five o'clock, twelve-year-old Eugene Barbadette was busy in his father's barn helping to prepare animal feed. He looked out the open barn door and saw a beautiful lady in the air, about twenty feet above the roof and between two chimneys of a neighbor's home. The lady was wearing a dark blue dress covered with gold stars, a black veil, blue shoes with gold buckles, and a simple gold crown. Eugene stood there entranced for a few minutes.

His father and brother, ten-year-old Joseph, came out from the barn. Eugene called out, "Look over there, above the house. Do you see anything?"

Joseph replied, "Yes, a beautiful lady dressed in blue." He described the lady the same way Joseph had seen her. Their father did not see her, so he ordered the boys to return to feeding the horses.

A little later, the father told the boys to go out and look again. The lady was still there. Their mother, Victoria Barbadette, arrived. Knowing the boys were honest and did not lie, she said it may be the Blessed Mother Mary who appeared to them. Victoria assembled the family, and they began to pray the Lord's Prayer and Hail Mary five times together. The brothers were very pious. They began each day reciting the Rosary for the intentions of their older brother, serving in the French army. (Praying for the intentions of another means praying for someone and adding the power of your prayer to whatever they are praying for.)

Victoria called to a nun from the convent next door. The nun came over, bringing two little children, Francoise and Jean-Marie, with her. As they prayed the Rosary, the children saw the garment's stars multiply until it was almost entirely gold. The little children immediately clapped with excitement and called out, "Oh, look at that lovely lady with the golden stars!"

Sister Marie Edouard joined the group. After hearing the little children describe seeing a lady, she ran back to bring Father Guerin and another child, six-year-old Eugene Friteau. Eugene also saw the lady.

About fifty villagers were now gathered near the barn. Augustine Boitin, just two years old, reached out to the lady and said, "The Jesus. The Jesus." Only these six children would see the apparition. Mary's eyes, displaying unutterable tenderness, were fixed on the children.

Father Guerin asked everyone to pray, so they all knelt and prayed the Rosary. Sister Marie Edouard led the crowd in reciting the Magnificat, also called Canticle of Mary, which is taken from Luke's Gospel (1:46–55). It is the Blessed Virgin Mary's hymn of praise to the Lord.

Gradually, a message in gold letters on a white streamer appeared to be unfolding in the sky: "Pray my children." All the children saw the same message. The message continued to unfold: "God will answer your prayers very soon. He will not allow you to be touched. My Son allows himself to be moved with compassion."

Father Guerin led the crowd in singing a hymn of praise to Jesus. Mary's expression changed to sadness. When the song ended, a red cross with the wounded body of Christ appeared before the Virgin, who held it. At the top, in large red letters, was written, "Jesus Christ." At eight thirty that night, the people sang, "Ave, Maris Stella," and the crucifix disappeared. Mary smiled, and two small white crosses appeared on her shoulders. She lowered her hands, and a white veil gradually covered her, from foot to crown.

At about eight forty-five, the children announced, "It's over. Our Lady has disappeared."

The apparition lasted about three hours.

During the apparition, General Karl von Schmidt received orders from the Prussian high command to halt his campaign and withdraw. Ten days later, an armistice was signed between France and Prussia at Versailles. The miraculous intercession of Blessed Mary had saved Pontmain.

OUR LADY OF PONTMAIN

The Bishop of Laval initiated an investigation into the apparition, and witnesses were interviewed. The visionary children were interrogated intensely. On February 2, 1872, Bishop Wicart issued a pastoral letter giving authenticity to the apparition.

In May 1872, Bishop Wicart authorized construction of a sanctuary at the site of the apparition. It was consecrated in 1900. The church is a magnificent structure. Pope Pius X elevated the sanctuary to the status of a basilica in 1905. Approximately two hundred thousand people visit Our Lady of Pontmain each year.

Joseph Barbadette became a priest of the Congregation of the Oblates of Mary Immaculate. His brother, Eugene, became a diocesan priest. Eugene was assisted by one of the female visionaries as his housekeeper. Another visionary, Jeanne-Marie Lebosse, became a nun.

KEY MESSAGES FROM BLESSED MARY

With motherly love and compassion, Mary visits the faithful in their times of need to avoid the wrath of war. Mary encourages them to pray. She promises that God will answer their prayers and reminds them that they will remain safe from the war. Using an apparition, Mary shows the faithful the wounded body of Jesus Christ on a red cross.

CHAPTER 13
1877: APPARITION IN GIETRZWALD, POLAND

During his first decade as king of Prussia, Kaiser Wilhelm I successfully unified the German-speaking countries after going to war with Denmark, Austria, and France. In 1871, the king accepted the new title of German emperor. He built a majority coalition of supporters by excluding Catholics.

Kulturkampf is a German name given to the conflict between the government of Prussia and the Roman Catholic Church. It was a political struggle for the rights and self-government of the church over control of educational and ecclesiastical appointments. As a result, the Polish language was banned in all schools. Many Catholic priests and congregations were removed from the Warmia region in northern Poland. Kulturkampf lasted from 1871 until 1878.

THE APPARITION

In the village of Gietrzwald, Poland, on June 27, 1877, thirteen-year-old Justyna Szafrynska was walking home from catechism class with her mother, prior to receiving her First Holy Communion, and Justyna heard Angelus bells. (These bells ring out to remind Catholics to say a devotion commemorating the Incarnation, the moment when Jesus was conceived.) She looked up and saw a bright light and a figure dressed in white on a nearby maple tree. The figure was seated on a gold, pearl-studded throne. Then, Justyna saw the glowing figure of an angel, in white with golden wings, descending from heaven. When Justyna prayed the Hail Mary, the figure on the throne rose and ascended into heaven with the angel.

Justyna's mother never saw the apparition. She encouraged Justyna to speak with the parish priest about what she saw. The priest recommended she visit the apparition site again the next day. Justyna did as she was told, but she took her friend, twelve-year-old Barbara Samulowska, with her.

This time, Angelus bells rang out again. The maple tree became brightly illuminated. A golden circle appeared with a throne of gold. Two angels escorted the Blessed Mother to the throne. When Mary was seated, two other angels brought baby Jesus in a heavenly glow and placed him on Mary's left knee. The baby was holding an orb in his left hand. Other angels raised a crown above Mary's head. Another angel brought a gold scepter and held it in its right hand above the crown. One more angel hovered above the scene and pointed to a cross.

Both girls saw the apparition and asked, "Who are you?"

The lady replied, "I am the Blessed Virgin Mary of the Immaculate Conception."

The girls said, "What do you require, Mother of God?"

She answered, "I wish you to recite the Rosary every day."

On June 30, Mary appeared on her own, without angels. During the month of July, Justyna and Barbara were visited daily by Mary during the evening Rosary service. The apparitions continued daily for almost three months, ending on September 16.

During the apparitions, the children asked many questions. They wanted to know about the health and salvation of different people—and if the church in Poland would be liberated. They asked if new priests would be assigned to parishes in Warmia.

Mary said, "Yes, provided people pray fervently. Then the church will not be persecuted, and the orphaned parishes will receive priests." Mary repeated that the girls should "pray the Rosary zealously."

HOLY WATER

On September 8, the girls were instructed to go to a nearby spring. Mary blessed the spring for the healing of both physical and spiritual maladies. Mary said, "Now, the sick people can take this water for their healing."

In early September, the bishop asked three physicians to examine the visionary girls during an apparition. The physicians reported the girls had slower pulses. Their upper and lower extremities got cooler. Their gazes were fixated.

Word of the apparitions spread throughout the region, and people flocked to the shrine. The Feast of the Nativity of the Blessed Virgin Mary on September 8 attracted fifty thousand pilgrims to the village of Gietrzwald. Pilgrims drew water from the spring, and miracle healings were reported. Each year, Gietrzwald attracted a greater number of pilgrims. Local priests expanded the shrine to accommodate them.

OUR LADY OF GIETRZWALD

With Kulturkampf and the increasingly difficult position of the Polish population in a Prussian state, the apparitions were powerful signs. They became a symbol of both Catholicism and Polish national spirit. A resurgence of moral living returned to the region. Many families began to pray the Rosary daily. More people desired to become priests and nuns.

In 1877, the bishop of Warmia, Filip Krementz, convened a commission of theologians and doctors to investigate the apparitions. The girls were interviewed and examined separately. The commission's forty-seven-page report recommended the Catholic Church authenticate the apparition.

The church in Gietrzwald was designated as a Basilica Minor by

Pope Paul VI in 1970. However, it was not until 1977, one hundred years after the apparitions, that they were finally authenticated by the bishop. On September 1, 1977, Cardinal Karol Wojtyla, then archbishop of Krakow and future Pope John Paul II, attended the celebration when Bishop Jozef Drzazga of Warmia officially validated the authenticity of the apparitions in Gietrzwald.

Both visionaries became nuns in the religious congregation of the Daughters of Charity of St. Vincent de Paul. They first joined in Chelmno, Poland, near Gietrzwald, and then moved to Paris, France. Barbara took a religious name, Sister Stanislawa, and left Paris for a mission in Guatemala. She died there on December 6, 1950, and was beatified on February 2, 2005.

Justyna left the congregation in 1897 and returned to lay life. In 1899, she married Raymond Etienne Bigot in Paris. It is not known where she is buried.

KEY MESSAGES FROM BLESSED MARY

During a period of religious persecution, where the freedom of religion is restricted by government officials, Mary visits to remind the faithful to pray. Prayer is more powerful than government officials. With more prayer and fervent prayer, God can change the hearts of powerful men and women with no faith.

Spring water blessed by Mary coupled with faith in God results in healing miracles. There is a revival of Christian faith, and many souls are saved.

CHAPTER 14
1879: Apparition in Knock, Ireland

Just like the town of Lourdes in France, Knock was also a small peasant town. It is located about sixty miles north of Galway, on the northwestern coast of Ireland. In 1879, potato farming was not going well due to heavy rains destroying the crops. A famine was feared. On Thursday, August 21, 1879, at approximately eight o'clock on a rainy night, an apparition appeared at a Catholic church in Knock.

Mary McLoughlin, the parish housekeeper, looked out the kitchen window and noticed a bright light. Through the pouring rain, she could see three figures standing in front of a wall. She thought they were replacement statues for ones that had been destroyed in a storm a year earlier.

Mary ran to the home of her friend, Margaret Byrne. After visiting for half an hour, Mary decided to leave. Margaret's sister agreed to walk with her. The two women passed the church and saw the figures. When they realized the figures were an apparition from heaven, Margaret's sister ran home to tell her family.

Word spread quickly through the small town. Soon there were fifteen people kneeling in the pouring rain, praying the Rosary. They ranged in age from a young boy, age six, to a lady in her seventies. They jointly recited the Hail Mary for nearly two hours, even though the younger townspeople only spoke English and the older townspeople only spoke Irish.

The apparition included, from left to right, Saint Joseph, the Blessed Virgin Mary, Saint John the Evangelist, and Jesus Christ. Christ was depicted by a lamb standing on an altar in front of a taller cross. Blurred heavenly beings were flying near the cross. Everyone in the apparition was wearing white clothing. Joseph, Mary, and John were positioned deferentially in the direction of Christ, the centerpiece of the apparition. An aging Joseph, father of the Church, kept his head bowed and his hands together prayerfully. Mary wore a gold crown with a golden rose in front. Her arms were outstretched in an upward position as she looked toward the heavens. John wore a bishop's hat and held a book of Gospels in his left hand and left forearm. His right arm was raised in the air as though he was teaching.

No one in the apparition spoke. Although it was raining extremely hard, the site around the apparitions remained dry. A farmer half a mile away reported seeing a bright light near the church.

In a time of great desperation for the people of Knock, a supernatural apparition pointed to the cross and God above for miraculous assistance. It reminded the faithful to read the scriptures, attend church services, and pray to their Savior for help and guidance.

OUR LADY OF KNOCK

Knock became a pilgrimage sight for spiritual healing and forgiveness. Many miracles of physical healing also occurred there. People left their crutches and canes. The local priest put up a sign asking everyone who was healed to let him know. The priest recorded over six hundred healings in his book, but none of the many early healings were submitted to the Vatican for verification.

Years later, a lady with multiple sclerosis went there to pray. Although normally bound to a wheelchair, she was brought to a healing and adoration service tied to a stretcher. After returning to her apartment, she asked to be unbound because she believed she could walk. She was healed of multiple sclerosis. The Vatican investigated this potential miracle. Thirty years later, they declared it a miracle. Because multiple sclerosis was a relatively new disease and medicines were unknown, they waited to be sure medicine was not the reason for her cure.

A formal inquiry into the apparition was set up by the local bishop and Ireland's Catholic hierarchy. Fifteen witnesses were interviewed separately by doctors and theologians. The Knock apparition was authenticated by the Vatican in 1879 and deemed worthy of devotion. Pope John Paul II visited the site in 1979 as his primary destination on a trip to Ireland.

A new church, Our Lady Queen of Ireland, was built in 1976. It holds two thousand people. More than half a million pilgrims visit Knock each year. A larger church is needed. Today at the Knock Shrine, there are Rosary processions like those at Lourdes. They also hold a Eucharistic adoration service. The church has fifty confessionals, and ten full-time priests and many guest priests volunteer their time. No one is asked how long it has been since they last went to confession. Just as in Lourdes, volunteers help transport infirmed visitors in wheelchairs and on gurneys.

KEY MESSAGES FROM BLESSED MARY

With motherly love and compassion, Mary visits the town of Knock when famine is feared. Without saying anything to the visionaries directly, Mary starts a revival of Christian faith in the community. The faithful begin to pray more often. After word of the apparition spreads, the faithful arrive from more distant locations to pray for healing miracles. Many healing miracles occur, and many souls are saved.

CHAPTER 15

1917: APPARITION IN FATIMA, PORTUGAL

Revolutionaries in Portugal overthrew the monarchy in 1910. Because the church was associated with the monarchy, anti-Catholicism raged throughout Portugal. Catholic churches and schools were seized by the government. Nearly two thousand priests and nuns were killed by anti-Christian groups.

World War I ravaged Europe from 1914 to 1918. Portugal tried to remain neutral at first, but it eventually joined the Allies. Unfortunately, 220,000 Portuguese civilians died during the war, many due to food shortages and the Spanish flu.

Fatima is a small village in central Portugal, about eighty miles north of Lisbon. It is a famous Catholic pilgrimage site that is, ironically, named after the daughter of Mohammed, the prophet of Islam. On the thirteenth day of each month, from May through October every year, nearly one hundred thousand pilgrims come to Fatima. As a personal sacrifice, many pilgrims walk from Lisbon. Some walk the last miles on their knees. Many other pilgrims pray the Rosary on the concrete plaza while walking on their knees.

Fatima plaza and Basilica of Our Lady.

LUCIA OF FATIMA

Lucia dos Santos is one of three visionary children in Fatima, Portugal. She was the youngest of seven children, born on March 22, 1907. Fatima was a town of peasants, and most mothers worked in the fields, but Lucia's family owned a large piece of property.

Lucia's mother was literate, but she never taught any of her children to read or write. She did teach the children the Holy Rosary and other prayers. Lucia's father was generous and hardworking. He liked to tell fairy tales and sing folk songs. Lucia received her first Holy Communion at the age of six, despite age ten being the standard. The family endured trials and misfortunes. Family circumstances forced Lucia to start tending sheep at age seven.

A MYSTERIOUS PRESAGE

In 1915, seven-year-old Lucia dos Santos was tending sheep with three companions. As noontime approached, they were hungry and decided to eat their lunch. Lucia invited her companions to pray the Rosary with her. Right after they started the prayer, a bright statue appeared in the air above the trees. The rays of light were so bright that they could not see the statue clearly. The girls finished their prayer, and the statue disappeared. Upon returning home, Lucia told her mother about seeing the bright rays of light and a bright statue, but she did not believe her.

One year later, in 1916, Lucia and her three companions were tending sheep in the same place. Once again, they saw a bright statue, yet they could not see any arms or legs. Lucia told her mother about the second vision. Her mother did not believe her and called it "childish nonsense."

APPARITIONS OF THE ANGEL

Lucia's cousins, Francisco and Jacinta Marto, wanted to tend sheep with Lucia and were given permission by their parents. Lucia then began tending sheep with her two cousins instead of her three companions. One day, after playing a game, the three children looked up and saw a bright light coming toward them from above the olive trees. As it drew closer, they saw it was a young man, about fifteen years old.

Lucia said he was the Angel of Peace. The angel knelt on the ground with his forehead also touching the ground and asked the children to say a short prayer with him. They repeated the prayer three times, and then he departed.

Later in the summer, they saw the young man again. Lucia said they were asked to pray very much and offer prayers and sacrifices to God. The children were requested to make of everything they can a sacrifice and offer it to God as an act of reparation for the sins by which he is offended and in supplication for the conversion of sinners. They will then draw down peace upon their country. The young man was a guardian angel: the Angel of Portugal.

Months later, the angel appeared for the third time. He was holding a chalice in his left hand. A Communion host was suspended above the chalice. Some drops of blood fell from the host into the chalice. Leaving the chalice suspended in air, the angel knelt beside the children and prayed for the conversion of sinners. The angel rose, took the chalice, and gave the host to Lucia. He let Francisco and Jacinta drink from the cup, and then he disappeared and never returned.

APPARITION OF MARY

On May 13, 1917, the same three shepherd children from Fatima were tending sheep. This time, they saw a bright light and an apparition of Mary, the mother of Jesus, standing near an oak tree. Lucia dos Santos was nine, Francisco Marto was eight, and Jacinta Marto was six.

Mary asked the children to pray the Rosary for world peace, for the end of World War I, for sinners, and for the conversion of Russia. Mary referred to herself as the "Lady of the Rosary." Mary promised the children she would return on the thirteenth day of each month for the next five months. In response to a question from Lucia, Mary said she came from heaven. According to Lucia, Mary wore a white mantle edged in gold and held a rosary in her hand. She appeared more brilliant than the sun.

Statue of Mary in Fatima.

MARY ASKED THE CHILDREN TO HELP SINNERS:

> Sacrifice yourself for sinners, and say many times, especially whenever you make some sacrifice: O my Jesus, it is for love of thee, for the conversion of sinners, and in reparation for the sins committed against the Immaculate Heart of Mary.

The children reported the apparition to their parents. Once again, no one believed their story. Lucia's mother forced Lucia to admit she was lying. Her sisters and brothers taunted her. Townspeople laughed at all three children. Even when interviewed by the priest, Lucia was told it may be the work of the devil. Lucia and the children were horrified. As the children thought about the message from Mary, they realized the scolding and taunting were part of the sacrifice they needed to make.

As the three children reported each successive apparition, the crowds grew larger. Only the children could see and hear Mary. Because of growing doubts and skepticism among local adults, Mary told the children she would let the townspeople know the children had seen a real apparition from God in several months, on October 13 at noon.

The town administrator gathered the three children and questioned them. He did not like their answers and placed the three children in jail. The administrator threatened to boil the children in oil until they died. In their jail cell, they prayed with the other inmates. The next day, after the children still refused to retract their story under threat of death, they were released.

As part of their sacrifice, the children gave up their lunch and fed it to the sheep. They also found some rope and tied it tightly around their waists until it hurt. Mary told the children their sacrifices were appreciated. However, she cautioned them not to wear the rope around their waists at night.

During the children's sixth and final apparition on October 13,

Mary repeated her request for the children to pray the Rosary daily. She also asked that a chapel be built at the apparition site to honor the Lady of the Rosary.

Lucia recounted that Mary left and then reappeared to the children with Joseph and the child Jesus. She left again and reappeared multiple times dressed as Mary under different titles: "Our Lady of Sorrows" and "Our Lady of Mt. Carmel." While the children watched the changing apparitions, the crowd saw something else.

DANCING OF THE SUN

Expecting to see a miracle from God on October 13 at noon, seventy thousand people arrived to watch the apparition. However, they could only see the children and not the apparitions. It had been raining, but the rain stopped, and the sky cleared. Because people came from areas with different time zones, there was confusion about the start time. The crowd grew restless and impatient—and then the sun began to change.

People could look easily at the sun without hurting their eyes. The sun seemed to flicker on and off. It moved from behind the clouds to spin and tremble for ten minutes. It moved in one direction, then another, and made terrifying plunges toward the earth. The sun shot rays in different directions and changed to different colors. The crowd was frightened by the unnatural movements of the sun.

After the sun returned to its normal position, the once-soggy crowd realized their clothes were completely dry. Several newspaper reporters were there to record and report the events. Many finally believed what the children reported, and October 13, 1917, became known as "the Day the Sun Danced."

PROMISE OF HEAVEN

In response to a question from Lucia during the first apparition, Mary said all three children would go to heaven when they died.

However, Francisco was told he must say many prayers. During the second apparition, Mary revealed that the two younger children would be taken to heaven soon, but Lucia would live longer. Due to a flu epidemic, Francisco died in 1919, and Jacinta died in 1920. Lucia grew up and became a Carmelite nun. She died in 2005 at the age of ninety-seven.

THE FIRST TWO PREDICTIONS

Throughout the six apparitions, Mary shared three secrets with the children. Lucia began to reveal the secrets in 1927. The first secret was a prediction that peace was coming—and World War I was ending. This prediction came true one year after the Day the Sun Danced.

The second secret was a prediction of the immense damage Russia would do to humanity by abandoning the Christian faith and embracing communist totalitarianism and atheism. Mary also spoke of trials that would afflict the world through war, starvation, and persecution of the church in the twentieth century unless the world made reparations for sins. This prediction presaged World War II, which came true more than twenty years later.

Mary also shared a vision of hell with the children to show that it really exists. Mary encouraged the church to pray that peace comes upon the world and trials be averted.

THE THIRD PREDICTION

The third secret was revealed by the Vatican in 2000. It referred to a "bishop in white" who is shot by a group of soldiers. Many people believe the third secret was about the assassination attempt on Pope John Paul II on May 13, 1981. The assassination attempt occurred two years after the pope's triumphant return to Poland, where he spent nine days speaking to crowds totaling six million people. John Paul could sense that the days of communism in Poland were numbered and religious freedom would be restored. Russian communist leaders feared John Paul's power over the masses.

As Pope John Paul II passed through the crowd in St. Peter's Square, he was shot four times. Two bullets became lodged in his lower intestine, and two passed through his hand and right arm, hitting two innocent bystanders. One bullet broke a bone attached to the base of the spine. It is a miracle that the bullet did not paralyze or kill quickly by piercing a major blood vessel or vital organ. If you refer to an anatomy book showing the area where the bullets were embedded, you will notice there is very little space for a bullet to pass through and miss so many vital organs.

The third secret by Mary came true sixty-four years after she first made the prediction. John Paul II also believed he was part of the third Fatima secret and credits a "Mother," Mary, with helping to guide the bullets in order to save his life. May 13, 1981, happens to be the sixty-fourth anniversary of the first apparition in Fatima. It is also the ongoing Feast of Our Lady of Fatima Day, a religious holiday in the Catholic Church since 1930.

The Fatima secret referred to a bishop. Although John Paul II was pope, he was also a bishop. All modern Catholic popes have two major responsibilities. One is to lead the world's Catholic church from the Vatican. The other is to be the Bishop of Rome. The Catholic Church has only two types of Holy Orders for clergy. One type of Holy Orders is for priests, which is the Christian sacrament of someone becoming a priest. The second type of Holy Orders is for bishops, which come from among the priests. Bishops are usually leaders of territorial units called dioceses. There is no third type of Holy Orders for archbishops, cardinals, or popes.

WARNING OF CHASTISEMENTS FOR THE WORLD

The three specific predictions, or prophesies, of Fatima have been fulfilled. However, on July 13, 1917, Mary communicated four chastisements to the visionaries if her requests went unheeded:

> God wishes to establish in the world devotion to my Immaculate Heart. If what I say to you is done, many souls will be saved and there will be peace. The [First World] war is going to end; if people do not cease offending God, a worse one will break out during the pontificate of Pius XI. When you see a night illuminated by an unknown light, know that this is the great sign given you by God that he is about to punish the world for its crimes, by means of war, famine, and persecutions of the church and of the Holy Father. To prevent this, I shall come to ask for the consecration of Russia to my Immaculate Heart.

The four chastisements are war, famine, persecution of the church, and persecution of the Holy Father:

> If my requests are heeded, Russia will be converted, and there will be peace. If not, she will spread her errors throughout the world, causing wars and persecutions of the church. The good will be martyred, the Holy Father will have much to suffer, and various nations will be annihilated. In the end, my Immaculate Heart will triumph. The Holy Father will consecrate Russia to me, and she will be converted, and a period of peace will be granted to the world.

MARY'S CHASTISEMENT PREDICTION REPEATED THREE HUNDRED YEARS LATER

In Quito, Ecuador, in 1610, Mary predicted a "spiritual catastrophe" that would start with modernism in the nineteenth century and occur shortly after the middle of the twentieth century. The "spiritual catastrophe" included the following:

- widespread moral corruption
- contempt for the sacrament of holy matrimony
- depraved priests who will scandalize the faithful and cause suffering for good priests
- unbridled lust that will ensnare many souls
- loss of innocence among children and loss of modesty among women
- lack of priestly and religious vocations

Mary called the world to conversion. Mary called believers to pray for the conversion of sinners. Failing to follow her request, the world would suffer chastisement during the middle to late twentieth century.

Again, in Fatima in 1917, Mary urgently called the world to conversion. She said failure to convert would result in a great chastisement, including annihilation of some nations. Mary's message remains the same as it was three hundred years earlier in Quito. However, there is more urgency this time.

THE POPE IGNORED THE REQUEST

Twelve years after Fatima, on June 13, 1929, Lucia reported that while praying she experienced a vision in which Blessed Mary said it was God's will that the pope, in union with all the bishops in the world, consecrate Russia to her Immaculate Heart. However, Pope Pius XI failed to follow the request, which would have mitigated the four chastisements. The faithful also failed to offer sufficient prayers as Mary previously requested. The four chastisements on the world in the twentieth century began ten years later.

A NIGHT ILLUMINATED BY AN UNKNOWN LIGHT

The night illumination sign from God, which warns of impending chastisements, occurred on January 25, 1938. Pius XI was pope of the Catholic Church at the time. The sky across western Europe, including areas going west to Bermuda and southeast to Australia, turned bloodred. The sight of the Great Aurora struck fear into the hearts of millions. News agencies across the world reported on this significant event. It occurred just as Mary predicted.

THE CHASTISEMENT OF WAR IN THE TWENTIETH CENTURY

It was the deadliest war in the history of humanity. The world experienced World War II, a global war that lasted from 1939 to 1945. There were seventy million to eighty-five million fatalities. The war inflicted a genocide on fifteen million people, including six million Jews.

Much of Europe was annihilated. Cities were laid waste, and the countryside was charred. Roads were pitted with shell holes. Rail lines and bridges were destroyed. Harbors were filled with sunken ships. Germany lost seven million people, which was 8 percent of the country's population.

More than half of the world's total fatalities were in the two atheist countries of the Soviet Union and China. The Soviet Union lost seventeen million people directly due to war and another eight million people due to famine and disease. China lost twenty million people due to war. Many atheist souls were lost to hell for eternity.

THE CHASTISEMENT OF FAMINE IN THE TWENTIETH CENTURY

It was the deadliest famine in the history of humanity. From 1959 to 1961, fifteen million people in China died from starvation in the Great Chinese Famine. Chairman Mao ordered millions of peasant farmers to work in the iron and steel industry. He radically changed farming regulations to eliminate ownership of farm property. The result was an insufficient food supply for the masses. It was the greatest human-made disaster in the history of the world.

THE CHASTISEMENT OF PERSECUTION OF THE CHURCH IN THE TWENTIETH CENTURY

The official religion of ninety million people changed from Catholicism to atheism in August of 1945. Following World War II, the Central European countries of Slovakia, the Czech Republic, Hungary, Bulgaria, Romania, East Germany, and Poland were placed under the communist and atheistic control of the Soviet Union. Religion was suppressed.

Parents were forced to choose between attending church or feeding their families. They were forced to choose between religion or high school educations for their children. Most parents chose to support their families and stopped attending church. A few risked their families' lives to secretly baptize infants in their home during the middle of the night. After several generations under communist control, religion largely disappeared. Children and grandchildren were raised away from the church. Except for Poland, the religious population of each country fell from 90 percent Christian to 10 percent Christian.

With guidance from Poland's Catholic leadership, Poland's twenty-four million people believed if everyone defied communist orders and attended church, they would not be punished. The Polish people understood the Soviets needed workers to make a communist economy work. They could not punish everyone. So the Polish population continued to attend church weekly while under Soviet control. The plan succeeded in Poland—but not in any of the other Central European countries.

Late-twentieth-century ethnic cleansing wars, like those in Rwanda and Yugoslavia, targeted religious people for slaughter. Monasteries, convents, and churches were destroyed, taking the lives of many priests and nuns.

In the rest of the world, widespread sexual abuse of children by Catholic priests occurred over a forty-year period beginning in the 1970s. Approximately three thousand to four thousand priests were accused of child molestation. Bishops, archbishops, and cardinals hid the crimes by transferring troubled priests to new locations. The church paid substantial fines in criminal courts. Many faithful Christians left the church, and others stopped giving offerings.

THE CHASTISEMENT OF PERSECUTION OF THE HOLY FATHER IN THE TWENTIETH CENTURY

Pope John Paul II was shot four times on May 13, 1981 as he entered St. Peter's Square in Vatican City. Mehmet Ali Ağca was apprehended immediately and later sentenced to life in prison. With God's grace and the help of the Blessed Mother, John Paul survived. The pope later forgave Ağca for the assassination attempt. At the Pope's request, Ağca was pardoned by the Italian president, Carlo Azeglio Ciampi, and was deported to Turkey in June 2000.

BELATEDLY CONSECRATING RUSSIA TO THE IMMACULATE HEART OF MARY

In 1952, Pope Pius XII finally accomplished the consecration of Russia to the Immaculate Heart of Mary. However, he failed to do so in union with all the bishops of the world, and it was too late. The war was over, and atheism had already expanded.

Pope John Paul II recognized the past failures of the church. He also realized it was too late to follow the original instructions. John Paul II determined on his own that he should consecrate the entire world to Mary's Immaculate Heart. John Paul asked all the Catholic bishops of the church to join him in the consecration. He accomplished this on March 25, 1984, in St. Peter's Square. He arranged for the Fatima statue of Mary to be in the square at the time of his remarks.

Sister Lucia said the 1984 consecration was accepted by God. The Soviet Union peacefully collapsed seven years later, on August 22, 1991. In addition to the seven Soviet satellite countries in Central Europe being freed from atheism, fifteen former Soviet republics were also freed from atheism. The fifteen additional countries gaining religious freedom are Russia, Ukraine, Belarus, Moldova, Estonia, Latvia, Lithuania, Armenia, Azerbaijan, Georgia, Kazakhstan, Kyrgyzstan, Tajikistan, Turkmenistan, and Uzbekistan. In total, more than 340 million people were peacefully freed from forced atheism because of prayer unleashing the power of the Holy Spirit.

Russia officially returned to the Christian faith. Today, daily prayer and Christian instruction are required in Russian public schools. Russian leaders may strive to expand their territory—but not with the intent of forming new atheist societies. Yet, the world must still recover from the past spread of atheism in Central Europe and the former Soviet republics. Much prayer and penance are needed to save the souls remaining at risk there.

The twentieth-century chastisements occurred as predicted by Mary, both in Quito in 1610 and in Fatima in 1917. However, one promise from her Quito message remains. Without giving a timeline, Mary promises to throw Satan into the infernal abyss.

POPE JOHN PAUL II'S REMARKS ON THE MEANING OF CONSECRATION

In a homily given in Fatima on May 13, 1982, Pope John Paul II explained the meaning of consecration to the Immaculate Heart of Mary:

> The heart of the Blessed Mother … calls us. She not only calls us to be converted; she calls us to accept her motherly help to return to the source of redemption. Consecrating ourselves to Mary means accepting her help to offer ourselves and the whole of humanity to him who is holy, infinitely holy …
>
> God's holiness showed itself in the redemption of individuals, of the world, of the whole of humanity,

and of the nations: a redemption brought about through the sacrifice of the cross. *For their sake I consecrate myself,* Jesus had said (John 17:10).

By the power of the redemption, the world and humanity have been consecrated. They have been consecrated to him who is infinitely holy. They have been offered and entrusted to love itself, merciful love.

The mother of Christ calls us, invites us to join with the church of the living God in the consecration of the world. In this act … all of humanity, the nations and each individual person are presented to the eternal Father with the power of the redemption won by Christ. They are offered in the Heart of the Redeemer which was pierced on the cross.

OUR LADY OF FATIMA

At the Fatima worship site is a large plaza. On the left side of the plaza, there is a small Chapel of Apparitions and a statue of Mary as she appeared to the three children. At the top of the plaza lies the Basilica of Our Lady of the Rosary of Fatima. The basilica was built between 1928 and 1953, and it seats eight thousand people. All three visionaries are buried inside the front of this basilica. At the bottom of the plaza is the Basilica of the Holy Trinity, which was completed in 2007 and holds nine thousand people. On the right side of the plaza, there is a museum. In it is Mary's crown with a bullet attached. The bullet was gifted by John Paul. It was the bullet Mary guided through John Paul's body to save his life.

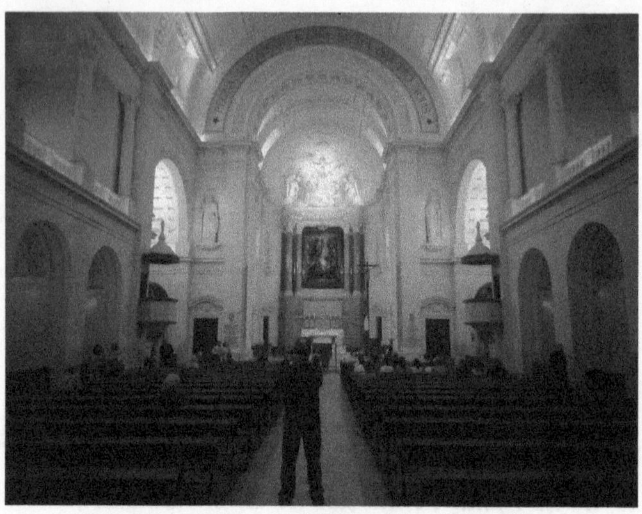

The Basilica of Our Lady of the Rosary of Fatima.

The Fatima apparition was approved by the Vatican on October 13, 1930. Approximately four million people visit Fatima each year. Many go there to pray for world peace and for sinners, as Mary requested, and there are also reports of physical healings. Many unbelievers are healed when Christian loved ones pray and use soil or water from Fatima on their ailing body parts. The miracle healings are both physical and spiritual.

KEY MESSAGES FROM MARY

With motherly love and compassion, Mary urgently asks the faithful for more prayer. Prayers can end wars and prevent future wars from being fought. Prayers can prevent famines, convert atheists to the Christian faith, and stop spiritual catastrophes. Because God performs miracles for those with faith, prayer is powerful.

Mary warns of future chastisements unless the faithful pray more and pray fervently. Prayer can either eliminate or mitigate the chastisements. Mary was especially concerned about Russia expanding atheism to other countries.

CHAPTER 16
1932: Apparition in Beauraing, Belgium

Beauraing is a small town in southern Belgium where the people speak French. Between November 29, 1932, and January 3, 1933, Mary appeared to five children. The children came from two families, who like many in the town, were no longer particularly religious. The Socialist Party, which was opposed to the church, won most of the local elections.

Three of the children were from the family of a railway clerk and his wife. They were fifteen-year-old Fernande Voisin, fourteen-year-old Gilberte Voisin, and thirteen-year-old Albert Voisin. Two girls were from the family of a farmer's widow. They were fifteen-year-old Andree Degeimbre and nine-year-old Gilberte Degeimbre.

On the evening of November 29, 1932, four of the children—Fernande, Gilberte, Albert, and Andree—were walking to the convent school to pick up the youngest child, Gilberte Degeimbre, who had stayed until six thirty to study.

While waiting for the convent front doorbell to be answered, Albert looked toward a railroad bridge just past the school and saw the luminous figure of a lady dressed in white clothes, walking on air just above the bridge. When the young Gilberte came to the door, all five children could see the apparition.

Upon seeing the apparition, the children moved closer. The lady seemed to be around nineteen years old with deep blue eyes. She had a rosary hung from her arm.

Albert asked, "Are you the Immaculate Virgin?" The lady smiled and nodded her head affirmatively. She told the children to "always be good."

Over the next few evenings, the children saw Mary by a hawthorn tree near the convent grotto. They knelt on the street and peered through the bars of the convent gate. At each apparition, the children would simultaneously drop to the ground on their knees very hard. Bystanders were concerned that the children may have injured themselves, but the children felt nothing. People also noticed the visionaries spoke with high-pitched voices when they prayed on their knees.

The children's parents did not believe their reports about Blessed Mary. Gilberte Degeimbre's mother made the girls eat separately in their rooms and refused to give them a hug at night because "they were lying." At the convent, Mother Theophile did not believe the children either. She locked the gate and kept two mean dogs inside the fence to prevent the children from returning. The local bishop ordered priests to stay away from the site.

The apparitions continued to appear before the five children. They saw a beautiful lady holding her hands in prayer with rays of light around her head. Although the apparitions did not occur every night, the children always met faithfully to pray the Rosary. When Mary did appear, the children dropped to their knees in unison.

On Thursday, December 8, the feast of the Immaculate Conception, a crowd of fifteen thousand people came to see a miracle apparition. However, they only saw the visionary children in ecstasy. The people were unable to see Mary. Church authorities arranged for physicians to test the children when they were in ecstasy. One child had a fire held under her arm. Another had their arm pinched very hard. A third child had a knifepoint pushed against them. None of the children noticed or felt what had happened. When examined immediately after the apparition, there were no marks on any of them. The children were questioned separately about details of what they saw.

On December 29, Fernande saw the Blessed Virgin with a heart of gold surrounded by rays of light. Two other children saw the heart of gold the next day.

Mary said, "Pray, pray very much." On January 1, Mary told Gilberte Voisin to "pray always." The next day, Mary told the children that she would speak to them individually on the following day.

On January 3, a crowd of thirty thousand people assembled as the children began to pray the Rosary. Mary appeared for the final time. To Gilberte Voisin, she said, "I will convert sinners." To Andree, she said, "I am the mother of God, the queen of heaven. Pray always."

Mary disappeared. Then with a loud noise like thunder and a ball of fire on the hawthorn tree, which everyone in the crowd could hear and see, Mary reappeared to Fernande. Mary asked her if she loved her Son and herself.

Fernande said she did.

Mary said, "Then sacrifice yourself for me." Mary glowed with extra brilliance, extended her arms, said goodbye, and disappeared.

OUR LADY OF BEAURAING

There were many conversions to the church. In 1935, the bishop of Namur appointed a commission to investigate the apparitions and related events. The apparitions were authenticated by the bishop on July 2, 1949. The bishop of Namur also authenticated two miraculous healings through the intercession of Our Lady of Beauraing, which occurred in the months following the last apparition. Pope John Paul II visited Beauraing on May 18, 1985.

All five visionaries married and lived quiet lives with their families. The last living visionary, Gilberta Degeimbre, died on February 10, 2015, at ninety-one.

REFLECTIONS OF A VISIONARY

When the youngest visionary, Gilberta Degeimbre, was eighty-five years old, she participated in a video interview about the apparitions. Gilberta clarified that when they knelt in front of Mary, it was involuntary, like someone was pushing down on their shoulders. Their knees hit hard on the ground, but it did not hurt. One picture shows her stockings ripped at the knee from the force.

When asked why she thought Mary appeared in Beauraing, Gilberta shared that Mary answered that question by saying, "So people will come here on a pilgrimage." Gilberta also noticed Mary would speak using as few words as possible.

Gilberta said Mary ended each apparition the same way. Mary held her hands in front of herself, as though in prayer, and she would slowly open her arms and disappear into a cloud.

Gilberta said that they had indescribable joy in the presence of Mary. "Mary loves us." Gilberta felt she was in the light. When Mary left, it was immediate darkness, with no transition. Gilberta greatly missed the feelings of ecstasy.

KEY MESSAGES FROM BLESSED MARY

With motherly love and compassion, Mary visits Beauraing after most of the faithful stop being particularly religious. She reminds the once faithful to pray more. Without prayer, even the faithful will lose their faith in Christ and vote for political leaders who are opposed to the church. Mary starts a revival of the Christian faith. She tells the faithful to pray always. Mary came to revive the church and to convert sinners.

CHAPTER 17

1945: Apparition in Amsterdam, Netherlands

Ida Peerdeman was born in Alkmaar, Netherlands, on August 13, 1905. She was the youngest of five children. On March 25, 1945, at age thirty-nine, Ida saw her first apparition of Mary, the mother of God, in Amsterdam. World War II was nearing its end. Between 1945 and 1959, Mary appeared to Ida fifty-six times. During some of the apparitions, Mary shared predictions of future wars and world events.

MARY REQUESTS VATICAN APPROVAL OF A FIFTH MARIAN DOGMA

During the first apparition with Ida on March 25, 1945, Mary requested her vocation be officially recognized by the Vatican as "Co-Redemptrix, Mediatrix, and Advocate." Mary promised that as the "Lady of All Nations" she would "give peace, true peace, to the world." She said, "The Father and Son sent me to save the world from catastrophe under this vocation."

Mary also described to Ida how her image should appear:

> I am standing on a globe, and both my feet are set upon it firmly. You also see my hands clearly as well as my face, hair, and veil. The rest is as in a haze. Now, I will explain to you why I come in this form. I stand as the Lady before the cross—with head, hands, and feet of a human being—but with the body, however, of the Spirit, because the Son came through the will of the Father. The Father and Son want to bring me into the world as Co-Redemptrix, Mediatrix, and Advocate. This will be the new and final Marian dogma. This image will precede. This dogma will be much disputed, yet it will be carried through.

The first Marian dogma is Mary is the mother of God. The second is perpetual virginity. The third Catholic dogma is Mary was conceived without original sin, the Immaculate Conception. The fourth dogma is Mary's body and soul were assumed into heaven, her Assumption.

MARY'S PREDICTIONS

During the first apparition on March 25, 1945, Mary also gave Ida the date of May 5. She showed her the rosary and said, "It is thanks to this." Next, Ida saw a vision of Allied soldiers. Mary said, "These will soon go home." A little more than a month later, on May 5, 1945, Allied forces liberated the Netherlands from Nazi occupation.

On April 21, 1945, Ida saw a vision of people fleeing. Mary told her it was Jews fleeing Egypt and that Israel would rise again. Mary said, "Yahweh is ashamed of his people." Three years later, on May 14, 1948, Israel became an independent country. However, because a large portion of its society is secular, it brings shame.

On October 7, 1945, Mary showed Ida a vision of China with a red flag. Four years later, Mao Tse-tung led communist forces in defeating nationalist forces. The People's Republic of China was formed and flew a red flag over its new capital in Beijing.

On August 30, 1947, Mary gave Ida visions of information sharing between the United States and the Vatican, which would occur decades later. Just as Mary predicted, President Ronald Reagan secretly shared US intelligence on Russian Communism with Pope John Paul II decades later during the 1980s.

On December 16, 1949, Ida saw a vision of a sign with the numbers "50-51-53" written on it. Mary told her there would be a war and disaster. It was the foretelling of the Korean War which occurred from 1950 to 1953. Later, Mary told Ida, "The fighting in Korea is a sham and the start of a great misery. But this will not last long. The Eastern peoples have been roused by a type of humanity which does not believe in my Son."

On December 31, 1951, Mary shared another prediction with Ida: "After much fighting, China will return to Mother church." This prediction has not yet come true. China remains an atheist state. However, the communist government allows a small minority of Chinese Catholics to attend Mass, contingent on government selection of bishops.

A PRAYER TO SAVE THE WORLD FROM CATASTROPHE

On February 11, 1951, Mary shared a prayer with Ida for the faithful of the world to pray:

> Lord Jesus Christ, son of the Father, send now your Spirit over the earth. Let the Holy Spirit live in the hearts of all nations. That they may be preserved from degeneration, disaster, and war. May the Lady of All Nations, who once was Mary, be our Advocate. Amen.

This prayer is given for conversion of the world. Mary directed that it should be made known throughout the world and prayed every day. Mary said, "Do pray in front of the cross."

On April 2, 1951, Mary said, "The world is not saved by force; the world will be saved by the Spirit. See that my prayer is made known throughout the world, among all nations. They all have a right to it. I assure you that the world will change."

On May 10, 1953, Mary instructed Ida to ask the pope to adopt the fifth and final Marian dogma and announce it to the world. "The time is now." Mary was sent by her Lord and Creator to deliver the world from a great catastrophe under this dogma. She wants her prayer and image spread together worldwide.

OUR LADY OF ALL NATIONS

On May 31, 1996, Bishop Bomers and Bishop Punt of Haarlem authorized public devotion and approval of the messages. Two months later, on June 17, 1996, Ida passed away at age ninety. Then on May 31, 2002, after concluding an investigation, Bishop Punt declared the apparitions to be "of a supernatural origin."

ACTIONS ON A POTENTIAL FIFTH MARIAN DOGMA

The fifth Marian dogma is not yet approved by the Vatican. On at least seven occasions, Pope John Paul II referred to Our Lady as the human Co-Redemptrix, with Jesus as the Divine Redeemer. John Paul also referred to Mary as Mediatrix, Advocate, and Our Lady of All Nations. Since 1983, eight million petitions were sent by the faithful to recent popes requesting they declare the fifth Marian dogma. The dogma was endorsed by six hundred bishops and seventy cardinals.

In April 2020, six cardinals and bishops from the five continents sent a respectful letter to Pope Francis recommending he proclaim the fifth Marian dogma. They cite John Paul's remarks in the letter.

They claim a papal proclamation would unleash graces and peace across the world. Vatican leadership has not yet acted on the request.

KEY MESSAGES FROM BLESSED MARY

Out of love and compassion, Mary visits Amsterdam to ask the faithful to pray a special prayer every day for the Holy Spirit to live in the hearts of all nations. If all nations come to Christ, there will be no more war—and many atheists will convert to Christianity.

Mary accurately predicts future wars and world events. One remaining prediction is that China will return to the Mother church after much fighting. Mary also asks the Catholic pope to declare the fifth and final Marian dogma to save the world from catastrophe. This request remains unfulfilled.

CHAPTER 18

1948: Apparition in Lipa, Philippines

Approval of the Marian apparition in Lipa is perhaps the most confusing decision by the Catholic Church of all thirty-four approved apparition sites. Following the first investigation, the local bishop declared the Lipa apparition "non-supernatural" and banned the site from veneration and visitation by the Church. The Vatican supported the negative decision. Decades later, the local archbishop lifted the ban and ruled the apparition site was now approved for veneration and visitation. Then, the Vatican quickly confirmed the original negative decision. However, in support of the local archbishop, the Vatican allows veneration and visitation at the Lipa site.

THE APPARITION

At 5:00 p.m. on September 12, 1948, a twenty-one-year-old postulant, a candidate who was seeking admission into a monastery or a convent as a religious vocation, saw an apparition. Teresita Castillo, also known as Sister Teresing, was in the process of becoming a Catholic nun in a Carmel monastery in Lipa, Philippines. Teresing walked out to the garden and saw a vine shake with no wind. She looked up and saw a radiant lady, as bright as the sun, standing before her.

The lady said, "Fear not, child. Kiss the ground. Whatever I tell you, you must do for fifteen consecutive days. Come again tomorrow and visit me in this spot."

The next day, September 13, Teresing returned to the same garden spot at 5:00 p.m. The lady appeared, holding a golden rosary on her right hand. Her dress was simple and pure white, held at the waist by a narrow cloth belt. The lady's feet were bare, and she was standing on a cloud floating just above the ground. Her face was beautiful and radiant. The lady told her to be faithful in coming there, whether in rain or sun. Teresing asked who she was. The lady replied, "I am your mother and the mother of my Son, Jesus." Then, she vanished.

On the morning of September 14, there was a shower of flower petals inside the monastery. The nuns awoke to petals in their rooms and at their doorsteps. At 5:00 p.m., Teresing returned to the garden spot.

Mary appeared with outstretched arms. She said, "I would like this place to be blessed tomorrow."

Teresing asked Mary at what time she preferred.

Mary answered, "Anytime Mother Cecilia wants."

After Mary vanished, Teresing went to tell Mother Cecilia what she had seen and heard.

A BLESSING

Mother Cecilia asked Bishop Obviar, an auxiliary bishop, to bless the garden at three o'clock the next afternoon. Before agreeing, the bishop requested proof that the apparition was supernatural. At that moment, Teresing became blind. A voice told Mother Cecilia to kiss the eyes of Teresing to cure her blindness. Mother Cecilia asked Bishop Obviar to come and see the proof he had requested. The bishop saw Teresing's blindness disappear and believed.

On September 15, the bishop, Mother Cecilia, Teresing, and all the Carmelite nuns attended the blessing ceremony. Mary appeared and was seen by everyone there except the bishop. Mary had a request for the Carmelite nuns: "Believe in me now, do not let the public know of my visit. Love one another as true sisters. Come and visit me often. Make this a sacred place."

When Mary vanished, large, very fragrant rose petals were scattered everywhere.

The bishop did not see the apparition, but he believed because of the rose petals.

Over the next fifteen days, Mary requested a statue to be made in her image. She told the nuns to describe to their bishop how they saw her and to make the statue as big as the Lourdes statue in the cloister.

Mary also said, "Pray the Holy Rosary every day. Believe and accept the graces given to you. I love you all very, very much. I shall always be with all of you."

On the last day of apparitions to the group of nuns, Mary said, "Love and obey your superiors. Remember the things I ask. Consecrate yourself to me on October 7. I am Mary, Mediatrix of All Grace." Later that day, a shower of rose petals continued both inside and outside of the convent. On October 7, thousands of rose petals filled the convent hallways and rooms.

WARNING OF A COMMUNIST INSURGENCY

On November 12, Teresing heard a small voice saying Mary was waiting for her in the garden. When Teresing arrived, Mary was radiant and beautiful, but she spoke with a touch of sadness:

> There will be persecutions, unrest, and bloodshed in your country. The enemy of the church will try to destroy the faith. Pray for the conversion of sinners throughout the world. Pray for those who rejected me, and for those who do not believe. I am saddened by the hardness of their hearts, but consoled by those

> who believe and trust me. Tell the people to pray the Rosary with devotion. Propagate the devotion to my Immaculate Heart. Spread the meaning of the Rosary because this will be the instrument for peace throughout the world. Do much penance for priests and nuns. But, be not afraid for the love of my Son will soften the hardest of hearts. What I ask here is the same as in Fatima. All these can now be revealed. I am Mary, the Mediatrix of All Grace. This is my last apparition here.

A communist rebellion was ongoing in the Philippines. The government of the Philippines was fighting against the New People's Army, which was the armed wing of the Marxist-Leninist-Maoist Communist Party of the Philippines. The Communist Party opposed religion and supported atheism. Teresing believed Mary's apparitions in Lipa would help the Philippines and start evangelization throughout Asia, including China.

News of the apparitions of Mary began to spread. Showers of rose petals occurred several times each week. Large groups of people began to visit the convent in Lipa daily to see the rose petals. Eyewitness reports from visitors stated the red rose petals were coming down from the clouds. The petals all moved together, from side to side, not straight down. As the petals fell onto the ground, they split into smaller petals. Some witnesses said they saw petals falling when no clouds were in the sky. Others said the falling petals were not affected by the wind or rain. Their motion and direction were unchanged. The rose petals only landed on the Carmel monastery grounds.

When scientists studied the petals, they reported that some petals displayed heavenly images including, Jesus, the Holy Family, and Mary. There were reports of many miracles of healing there. Some visitors applied a rose petal when praying for healing. Others used water, from a container with petals inside.

When Bishop Verzosa heard about the masses of people visiting the Carmelite monastery, he became upset. He had not been asked to approve the apparition or public announcements about it. The bishop ordered the statue of Mary to be relocated. When the bishop visited the convent and was met with a shower of rose petals, he fell to his knees and approved a return of the statue to its rightful place.

A special national novena (nine days of prayer) was held from May 22–31, 1949. The World Novena for Peace was held on October 5–13, 1950. There were numerous miracles and healings.

THE CHURCH RULES AGAINST

A committee of six local bishops was assigned to investigate the apparition reports. On April 12, 1951, the unanimous consent of the committee found the apparition to be non-supernatural. They ordered no petals to be given out. The statue was to be removed from public veneration. All visits were suspended.

The Carmelite nuns were ordered to burn all petals and documents, including Teresing's diary. There was deep sorrow and sadness among the nuns. The public made jeers and malicious insults. Supporting bishops were reassigned. Mother Cecilia was relocated. Teresing left the convent due to the stress of the investigations and worked at a church in Paranaque, Philippines. She remained silent on the apparition for forty-two years. The nuns remained silent and obedient, as Mary asked, and the statue was not seen in public for forty years.

In the 1980s, interest in the Lipa apparition was rekindled. Bishop Federico Escaler encouraged Mother Cecilia to speak about it. The Marian Research Center investigated the topic and interviewed public devotees who had seen the petals. Archbishop Gaviola talked with the Carmelite nuns personally and believed what he heard.

During the investigation, it was believed that no final decision from the Vatican was ever made, which made the bishop's commission decision easier and quicker to overturn. The archbishop ordered the statue placed back where it belonged and verbally lifted the 1951 order of the bishop's commission.

In 1992, June Keithley produced a documentary, *The Woman Clothed with the Sun*, which increased awareness among the public and devotees.

On Saturday, February 6, 1993, people came to the convent in droves to attend a Mass by the archbishop. The event was organized by laypersons, and there were twenty thousand to thirty thousand attendees, including many priests. Skies were cloudy that day. During Holy Communion, the archbishop heard the crowd applauding. When he looked up, he realized why.

DANCING OF THE SUN

The sun was dancing. The brilliance of the sun was softened, and it did not hurt anyone's eyes when they looked directly at it. Bright, colorful rays were extending outward. The sun flipped, turned, dropped, and then receded. It was a miracle of the sun.

The archbishop said, "Only Jesus mediates between God and humans; no one else can come between. In our belief, Jesus is assisted by his mother. It does not lessen his power. Instead, it multiplies it."

THE ARCHBISHOP CLARIFIES THE CONTROVERSY

The Catholic Church believes only Jesus mediates between God and humans. Mary's claim to be the Mediatrix of All Grace may be interpreted as Mary taking power from Jesus by unilaterally mediating Divine Grace on her own. However, the archbishop believes Mary only assists Jesus—with his permission. With this interpretation, the archbishop sees no conflict with church doctrine. However, other church leaders interpret it differently.

REPLICA PATRON SAINT

In 2002, Bishop Guillermo Afable became bishop in the neighboring Diocese of Digos, and he was installed in the Mary Mediatrix Cathedral. When the new bishop inquired about the history of the cathedral's patron saint, no one could explain. After further investigation, he discovered a previous Digos bishop was a friend of Bishop Obviar, who was reassigned following the 1951 order. The old Digos bishop ordered an exact replica of the statue of Mary from the same artist who made the statue for the Carmelite nuns. He disguised it with different colors, but the bishop renamed the cathedral Mary Mediatrix Cathedral.

Since 2004, the National Day of Prayer is celebrated in Lipa annually on September 12. Thousands of people come to celebrate with Our Lady, Mediatrix of All Grace.

THE CHURCH LIFTS THE BAN

On November 12, 2009, Archbishop Arguelles formally lifted the ban included in the 1951 decree. However, the Vatican reconfirmed its negative judgment. It is the only case in which the Vatican's official position on an apparition is negative, but veneration is permitted.

Several of the six bishops on the 1951 committee confessed on their deathbeds that they were threatened with excommunication unless they declared the apparition fraudulent.

Teresing Castillo was interviewed in 2011, sixty-three years after the apparitions. She stated that on ten different occasions between 1991 and 2000, she experienced a small shower of rose petals in Paranaque, where she still lived and worked. Teresing gave the petals to the Lipa convent for their use in healings. She was content with her life after placing the whole matter of apparitions in God's hands many years ago. Teresing Castillo passed away on November 16, 2016, at the age of eighty-nine.

KEY MESSAGES FROM BLESSED MARY

Out of motherly love and compassion, Mary visits a convent in Lipa. She lovingly speaks to the nuns. She asks them to love one another and to pray every day. Mary warns of a communist insurgency in their country that will try to destroy the church. She asks for more prayer for the conversion of atheists throughout the world. Mary came to save souls from going to hell.

CHAPTER 19

1968: Apparition in Zeitoun, Egypt

Apparitions of Mary were reported across the centuries with a single visionary or several visionaries. In Egypt, for the first time, Mary was seen by hundreds of thousands of people simultaneously. Over the duration of her visit to Zeitoun, as many as one million people saw her.

In June 1967, the Six-Day War between Israel and the Arab states of Egypt, Syria, and Jordan resulted in the loss of twenty thousand Arabs and eight hundred Israelis. Most of the losses were Egyptian. Borders between countries changed, and ownership of the Sinai Peninsula and Gaza Strip moved from Egypt to Israel. Relations between the Jewish state of Israel and many of their Arab neighbors had been difficult and volatile at times since the nation of Israel was formed in 1948.

THE APPARITION SEEN BY ONE MILLION PEOPLE

Less than one year after the war, on April 2, 1968, the apparition of a beautiful young woman was seen on top of St. Mary's Coptic Church in Zeitoun, a suburb of Cairo, Egypt. The apparition attracted a crowd, but it only lasted a few minutes. The following week, the apparition reappeared, and it continued two or three times per week for a total of three years, ending in 1971.

During the three-year period, approximately one million people saw the apparition. The largest crowd at one sighting totaled 250,000. Many prayed the Rosary. Witnesses included Orthodox, Catholics, Jews, Muslims, and foreign visitors.

Each apparition lasted from several minutes to nine hours. Witnesses reported seeing Mary holding an olive branch, a symbol of peace. She would bow in front of a cross and bless the crowds. Other witnesses reported seeing luminous doves flying at night and bright colors flashing. The smell of incense was in the air.

At times, Mary was seen with Joseph. At other times, she was hugging a young Jesus, who seemed to be around twelve years old. Throughout the many apparitions, Mary chose to say nothing, and she communicated only through gestures.

The press, including the *New York Times*, reported on the apparitions. Many photographs were taken of Mary standing on top of the church. One photograph showed her standing on air just above the church. She was illuminated in bright light and has a luminous dove above her head.

Many consider the apparitions to be Mary's return to Zeitoun. The Coptic Orthodox Church traditionally claimed that Zeitoun was one of the places where the Holy Family stayed during their flight to Egypt when Herod attempted to kill the child, Jesus.

A REVIVAL OF COPTIC CHRISTIAN FAITH

The apparitions caused a great revival of the Christian faith. Many conversions took place. Many miracles of physical healing near the apparition site were reported.

Because the Coptic Church had jurisdiction, they completed an investigation and determined the apparitions to be authentic. The Catholic Church accepted the determination of authenticity by the

Coptic Church. The Egyptian government completed their own investigation and reached the same conclusion.

A CATHOLIC EYEWITNESS

A representative of the Roman Catholic Church, who lived in Zeitoun, submitted a formal statement to the Vatican regarding his eyewitness accounts:

> The apparitions occurred on many different nights and are continuing in different forms. The Holy Virgin Saint Mary appeared sometimes in full form and sometimes in a bust, surrounded with a halo of shining light. She was seen at times on the openings of the domes on the roof of the church, and at other times outside the domes, moving and walking on the roof of the church and over the domes. When she knelt in reverence in front of the cross, the cross shone with bright light. Waving her blessed hands and nodding her holy head, she blessed the people who gathered to observe the miracle.
>
> She appeared sometimes in the form of a body like a very bright cloud, and sometimes as a figure of light preceded with heavenly bodies shaped like doves moving at high speeds. The apparitions continued for long periods, up to two hours and fifteen minutes as in the dawn of Tuesday April 30, 1968, when she appeared continuously from 2:45 a.m. until 5:00 a.m. Thousands of people from different denominations and religions, Egyptians and foreign visitors, clergy and scientists, from different classes and professions, all observed the apparitions. The description of each apparition as of

> the time, location and configuration was identically witnessed by all people, which makes this apparition unique and sublime.

There was no clear and specific message associated with the 1968 Marian apparitions in Zeitoun. However, with the Middle East in turmoil, it gave hope in a time of darkness. It also strengthened a faith in God for many.

KEY MESSAGES FROM MARY

After Egypt loses a war with Israel, Mary visits Zeitoun to share her love and compassion with the greater community. Without speaking directly to any visionary, Mary starts a revival of the Christian faith.

CHAPTER 20

1973: Apparition in Akita, Japan

Sister Agnes Sasagawa recently joined the Handmaids of the Eucharist, near the sea in northwest Japan. Members take vows of obedience, chastity, and poverty. They follow the examples set by the lives of Jesus and Mary by offering their lives to the service of God and neighbor. The sisters lead a quiet and hidden life centered on prayer.

Sister Agnes was forty-two years old and a convert from Buddhism. She was completely and incurably deaf. However, she was blessed with mystical graces.

On June 12, 1973, Sister Agnes saw brilliant rays of light emanating from the tabernacle in a convent chapel in Akita, Japan. (In the Catholic church, a tabernacle is an ornate box that holds consecrated Communion hosts.) This happened several times. The bishop and a priest also saw the light emanating from the tabernacle. On one of these occasions, Agnes saw angels surround the altar in adoration of the host.

A WOUND APPEARED ON HER LEFT HAND

On June 28, a cross-shaped wound appeared on the inside left hand of Agnes. The wound was painful and bled profusely. The wound disappeared on July 27 without leaving a trace.

While praying in the chapel on July 6, 1973, Agnes saw a bright light surround a wooden statue of Blessed Mary. Beneath her feet was a globe representing the world. The three-foot statue had been carved from a single block of wood.

Agnes heard a voice penetrating her deaf ears, and it said, "Your deafness will be healed." Nearly nine years later, on May 30, 1982, her hearing was fully restored.

THE STATUE OF MARY BLEEDS AND WEEPS

Later in the day on July 6, a few sisters saw drops of blood flowing from the statue's right hand. Blood flow repeated on four different occasions. On September 29, the wound on the statue disappeared. However, the statue began to sweat, especially on the forehead and neck.

Two years later, on January 4, 1975, the statue began to weep. It continued to weep occasionally during the following six years and eight months. During this time, it wept on 101 occasions.

MESSAGES FROM MARY

Agnes received a total of three messages from Mary. On July 6, Mary told Agnes her deafness would be healed. She asked Agnes to pray in reparation for the sins of man, by the suffering from the wound in her hand. Mary asked Agnes to "pray very much for the pope, bishops, and priests."

On August 3, Mary sent another message:

> Many people in this world afflict the Lord. I desire souls to console him to soften the anger of the

> Heavenly Father. I wish, with my Son, for souls who will repair by their suffering and their poverty for the sinners and ingrates. In order that the world might know his anger, the Heavenly Father is preparing to inflict a great chastisement on all humanity. With my Son, I have intervened so many times to appease the wrath of the Father. I have prevented the coming of calamities by offering him the suffering of the Son on the cross, his precious blood, and beloved souls who console him forming a cohort of victim souls. Prayer, penance, and courageous sacrifices can soften the Father's anger. I desire this also from your community … that it love poverty, that it sanctifies itself and prays in reparation for the ingratitude and outrages of so many people.

FIRE WILL WIPE OUT MUCH OF HUMANITY

On October 13, Mary spoke to Agnes for the third and final time.

> As I told you, if men do not repent and better themselves, the Father will inflict a terrible punishment on all humanity. It will be a punishment greater than the deluge, such as one never seen before. Fire will fall from the sky and will wipe out a great part of humanity, the good as well as the bad, sparing neither priests nor faithful. The survivors will find themselves so desolate that they will envy the dead. The only armaments which will remain for you will be the Rosary and the sign left by my Son. Each day recite the prayers of the Rosary. With the Rosary, pray for the pope, the bishops, and priests.

> The work of the devil will infiltrate even into the church in such a way that one will see cardinals opposing cardinals, bishops against bishops. The priests who venerate me will be scorned and opposed by their confreres ... churches and altars sacked: the church will be full of those who accept compromises and the demon will press many priests and consecrated souls to leave the service of the Lord. The demon will be especially implacable against souls consecrated to God. The thought of the loss of so many souls is the cause of my sadness. If sins increase in number and gravity, there will be no longer pardon for them.
>
> Pray very much the prayers of the Rosary. I alone am able still to save you from the calamities which approach. Those who place their confidence in me will be saved.

Blessed Mary warns the world of a life divorced from God. Yet, even with a crisis of faith, it is prayer, penance, and trust that can save humanity from this punishment.

CONCLUDING EVENTS

Approximately two thousand people witnessed tears flowing from the statue of Mary in Akita. Samples of tears and blood were examined in a university laboratory. Both were confirmed to be of human origin—but not connected to any known individual. The Vatican has never authenticated any weeping statue case. While most weeping statue cases were proven to be hoaxes by the Catholic Church, this case remains unproven. Unlike other cases, the entire nation of Japan saw the tears of this statue on national television.

On April 22, 1984, after eight years of investigations, Bishop

John Shojiro Ito of the Diocese of Niigata approved the "supernatural character of a series of mysterious events concerning the statue of the Holy Mother Mary" in Akita. The Vatican has not issued a formal statement on the matter, leaving it up to the local bishop's discretion.

KEY MESSAGES FROM MARY

Mary visits a nun in Akita to request prayers and reparation for the sins of humanity. Just as Mary warned in Amsterdam, she warns again in Akita of a great chastisement by fire on much of the earth. Only prayer and a sign left by Jesus will remain for the faithful. Mary's intercession with Jesus is the only remaining path to save the world from the approaching calamity.

CHAPTER 21

1981 Apparition in Kibeho, Rwanda

Rwanda is a country in central Africa that is best known for a civil war in 1994 that resulted in genocide. During a hundred-day period, from April 7 to July 15, approximately eight hundred thousand people were killed, out of a population of seven million. The government of the ruling Hutu tribe attempted to exterminate the minority Tutsi tribe. Neighbors killed neighbors. Some husbands killed their wives. Even priests and nuns were convicted of killing people, including some who sought shelter in the churches. The rulers required people to kill or be killed. The rest of the world did little to stop the genocide—even as they heard news reports and watched television video clips of the slaughter.

Kibeho is a small village in southwestern Rwanda. A sixteen-year-old girl, Alphonsine Mumurke, started to attend Kibeho High School, a boarding school, in October 1981. It was thirteen years before the civil war would begin.

THE APPARITION

On November 28, 1981, Alphonsine was working in the school cafeteria when she heard a voice. She stepped into the hall and saw a bright cloud forming into a beautiful lady, neither white nor black, floating above the floor. The lady was in a pool of brilliant and shimmering light. She wore a flowing seamless dress, and a veil covered her hair. She wore no shoes. Her hands were clasped in a gesture of prayer, and her fingers were pointing toward heaven.

Within a few seconds, Alphonsine dropped hard to her knees. She lost all control over her body. She had no sense of time or space, and she was oblivious to her surroundings. Alphonsine felt unimaginable joy and ecstasy.

Alphonsine asked the lady who she was.

The lady answered, "I am the mother of the Word."

Alphonsine recognized the lady as Mary, the mother of God.

Mary asked, "Of all things in heaven, what makes you happy?"

Alphonsine replied, "I love God and his mother who gave us their Son to save us."

Mary smiled and said, "It is true. I have come to assure you of this. I have heard your prayers. I would like it if your companions had more faith because some of them do not believe enough. I want people to trust and love me as a mother because I want to lead them to my Son, Jesus. Now, watch as I return to heaven to be with my Son." Then, Mary slowly rose and vanished.

Alphonsine fell to the floor and remained there in a semiconscious state for ten minutes. She saw her classmates trying to rouse her. Finally, Alphonsine regained full consciousness and stood up. When her classmates asked what had happened, she answered their questions. When Alphonsine reported what she saw, her teachers scolded her for lying. Her friends ridiculed her. Eventually the townspeople shunned her.

As Alphonsine was walking with a group of girls, she suddenly dropped hard to her knees and looked up peacefully. She saw Mary hovering above her in a soft but brilliant light. Only Alphonsine could see the apparition.

Mary began to share important messages for Alphonsine to deliver to Hutu government officials. Many Tutsis had been forced out of their homeland and were living as refugees, unable to return to their homes. Our Lady told Alphonsine that the government needed to "let the refugees come back," and there would be peace. Without that change, there would be too much hatred building between the tribes. Hutu officials were to stop discrimination against Tutsis, pray the Rosary daily, and follow the Ten Commandments.

HARASSMENT OF THE VISIONARY

While Alphonsine spoke with Mary, she was unaware of anyone else around her. The other girls laughed, waved their hands in front of Alphonsine's eyes, and shouted in her ears.

During another apparition, some of the girls threw their rosaries at Alphonsine. Others tried to land their rosaries on Alphonsine's head. A few of the more respectful girls politely laid their rosaries near the feet of Alphonsine. Mary asked Alphonsine to pick up the rosaries so she could bless them. Unaware of the girls around her, Alphonsine reached down and picked up some of the rosaries. Most of the rosaries stuck to the floor. Only the rosaries from the respectful girls were able to be lifted so Mary could bless them.

Near the end of each apparition, Mary would tell Alphonsine exactly when she would appear next. Local villagers, school officials, and other students would plan their schedules so they could attend. The local priest, who believed Alphonsine was a fake, encouraged one of the girls, Marie-Claire Mukangango, to heckle Alphonsine during the apparitions. Marie-Claire pulled Alphonsine's hair, pinched her, held a lighted candle under her arm, and stuck a long needle into her arm several inches deep.

Alphonsine never noticed. However, Alphonsine did ask Mary to allow others to see the apparition because she was weary from disbelief and ridicule. Some of the more faithful students also began to pray for Mary to reveal herself to others.

A SECOND VISIONARY

On January 12, 1982, Anathalie Mukamazimpaka, a pious seventeen-year-old girl, began to see Mary and receive messages. Anathalie was in her dormitory room with other girls, and everything went dark. A light illuminated the area with a background of colored flowers and floating crimson bubbles. A white sphere with intense light descended from above.

Anathalie heard a lady's saddened voice:

> I am sad because I have sent a message and no one will listen to the words as I desire. It is my wish for you to cry as you do now. Your tears are punishment, not because you have sinned against me, but to serve as a reminder that I can punish those who choose to ignore my messages. My child, you must pray, for the world is in a horrible way. People have turned from God and the love of my Son, Jesus. If you will work with me, I shall give you a mission to lead those lost souls back from the darkness.

Mary's messages stressed the importance of prayer, reflection, humility, and self-sacrifice. Mary then told Anathalie something she previously told Bernadette in Lourdes: "I cannot promise you happiness in this world, but I can promise you eternal happiness in the next world."

Anathalie reported the apparition. Some people believed both Alphonsine and Anathalie because two people were now reporting similar visions. Sensing the apparitions may be real, the priest told Marie-Claire to stop all harassment for now.

On March 1, 1982, Marie-Claire fainted during a walk in the garden. She awoke in a dark area with the smell of decaying flesh. It made her vomit. She remembered trying to run toward the school in the dark and crashing into the front door. As daylight returned, two classmates held her up in her drenched clothes. They told her a nun had thrown holy water on her to help revive her on the chapel floor. She went back to her dormitory room, only to see menacing beings approach and hover around her. Again, she awoke on the chapel floor.

Alphonsine gave her a little statue of Our Lady of Lourdes for protection. Alphonsine said the Blessed Mother had warned of plans by the devil to attack students at the school. The Blessed Mother said they could protect themselves by wearing their rosaries.

A THIRD VISIONARY

The next day in class, Marie-Claire felt strange. To avoid another blackout, she ran out of the room. She found herself on beautiful grass with a rainbow in the sky. A soft voice called, "Mukangango." Afraid it was another trick by the devil, Marie-Claire clenched her fists and said she was ready to fight.

The Blessed Mother laughed kindly:

> Why would you want to fight me, my child? What is making you so afraid? Never be afraid of your mother. There is no need to be afraid of them. I promise the things of the night that frightened you will not frighten you again. Sing a song for me using these words: Blessed are those who are persecuted because of righteousness, for theirs is the kingdom of heaven. Blessed are you when people insult you, persecute you, and falsely say all kinds of evil against you because of me.

Marie-Claire felt ashamed. She realized Mary was describing her own behavior toward Alphonsine. She refused to sing. So Mary brought in Anathalie to hold Marie-Claire's hand and help her sing.

Then Marie-Claire awoke again on the chapel floor, surrounded by thirty students who witnessed her singing to the Blessed Mother with Anathalie. Word spread quickly that Marie-Claire was now one of the few to personally experience an apparition. Marie-Claire's negative behavior vanished overnight.

During another apparition, Mary showed Marie-Claire a black rosary, the "Rosary of the Seven Sorrows." Mary taught her how to pray with it and asked her to eventually reintroduce it to the world. Tradition identifies seven sorrows of Mary, each one based off scripture passages. The seven sorrows are:

- the prophecy of Simeon
- the flight into Egypt
- the loss of Jesus in the temple
- Mary meets Jesus on the way to Calvary
- Mary stands at the foot of the cross
- Mary receives the dead body of Jesus
- Jesus's body is placed in the tomb

Marie-Claire asked Mary if her sister, who had died one year earlier, was in heaven.

Mary replied she was still in purgatory, waiting.

Marie-Claire said her family prayed for her often and asked if that was sufficient.

Mary explained, "Praying for your departed loved ones is of great comfort to them and of great help to the souls in purgatory, but people must still work to earn a place in heaven."

A few days later, Mary told Marie-Claire, "Today, your sister entered heaven and joined your father."

THE PRIEST'S CONVERSION

The local priest at the high school did not believe any of the girls who saw the apparitions. He wanted them all expelled from school.

Marie-Claire went to the priest with a message from the Blessed Mother because of his "unjust torment toward her children" and need to do penance. The priest was to kneel tonight, hold open his arms to God, and pray his Rosary three times.

That night, just to be safe, the priest locked his door and drew the curtains shut. As instructed, he knelt, held open his arms, and prayed the Rosary three times. Upon finishing, he placed the rosary in his nightstand, then placed some books and magazines on top of it before closing the drawer. The next day, he asked for Marie-Claire to visit to receive her punishment for asking that he pray the Rosary.

Marie-Claire arrived in a cheerful mood and said, "Father, the Blessed Mother is very pleased that you prayed your Rosary exactly as she asked you to, but she told me this morning that you shouldn't have piled all those books and magazines on the rosary when you put it back in the drawer. She says to keep it with you at all times and pray with it every day."

The priest was stunned by her words. He became an instant believer in the apparitions, and he fully supported the visionaries. The number of villagers visiting the school grounds continued to grow.

ALPHONSINE'S VISIT TO HEAVEN, PURGATORY, AND HELL

In recent years, Mary expresses alarm at how many atheists do not believe in heaven or hell. She began to show visionaries these places so they can personally testify to their existence. In Fatima, Mary showed visions of hell to three young visionaries. In Kibeho, she plans to take visionaries on a journey to see heaven, purgatory, and hell.

On March 20, 1982, Alphonsine took a "mystical journey" with Mary into another "world." She visited "places," which she described in symbolic language, that seemed like hell, purgatory, and heaven. However, Mary uses names for these places that are very different.

Before they left, Mary instructed Alphonsine to tell the school director "not to bury her, even if she appears dead." She would be gone for the entire weekend. During the eighteen hours in which this ecstasy took place, priests, nuns, nurses, and medical assistants for the Red Cross all saw that Alphonsine appeared to be in a deep sleep. She was rigid and her clasped hands could not be separated. They concluded that she was barely alive. Her breathing was one shallow breath each minute. Six men tried to roll her over but were unsuccessful.

Eighteen hours later, Alphonsine awoke responsive and with much energy and described her journey:

> The first place Mary took me was dark and very frightening, filled with shadows and groans of sadness and pain. She called it The Place of Despair, where the road leading away from God's light ends. Another place was filled with the golden light of happiness and laughter and songs sung by so many joyous voices. Mary explained that I could not see them while I was still living below. But one called out my name and said that she had been a visionary, too, and had been persecuted for her visions. But she joyfully urged me to have faith and confidence in the Blessed Mother, for she would protect me.

BETWEEN HEAVEN AND HELL

All Christians who die in God's grace are assured of eternal salvation. Some Christians who die can go directly to heaven. However, there is a belief that some Christians who die may need to undergo a period of purification before becoming holy enough to enter heaven. The place of purification is commonly called purgatory.

During the first 1,500 years of Christianity, beginning from the time of Christ, Christians believed in purgatory. After the Protestant

Reformation in 1517, Christians took different positions on whether purgatory exists between heaven and hell. Catholics believe in purgatory, and most Protestants do not.

Protestants base their views and beliefs solely on the Bible. They do not see any reference to the word *purgatory* in the Bible. However, after the Protestant Reformation, seven books from the Old Testament were removed from most Protestant's Bibles. These books are referred to as the *Apocrypha* and are included in the Roman Catholic Bible. One of the removed books, 2 Maccabees, contains the strongest reference to the concept of purgatory.

Catholics base their view of purgatory on both the Bible and tradition, from the time of Christ. In the *Apocrypha*, 2 Maccabees is the primary reference for the belief in purgatory. In 2 Maccabees 12:39–46, Judas Maccabeus and his military discovered that many of their fallen comrades carried sacred tokens of idols of Jamnia in their pockets, which was forbidden by Jewish law and a sin. Maccabeus believed the soldiers died as a punishment for their sin. Then, Maccabeus and his men prayed for God to forgive the sins of the dead soldiers. They also gathered a collection of money and sent it to Jerusalem as atonement for the dead soldiers' sins. These actions clearly indicate a purification was needed for the dead soldiers prior to their entering heaven.

C. S. Lewis believed in purgatory and wrote about it in several of his books. Lewis used his own method of reasoning, without reliance on a biblical basis, and he thought it was reasonable that some believers in Christ would need a period of purification in preparation for their everlasting home in God's presence.

DARKER APPARITIONS

On March 27, 1982, Marie-Claire received a more solemn message from Our Lady of Kibeho:

> The world is evil and rushes toward its ruin. It is about to fall in its abyss. The world is in rebellion against God. Many sins are being committed. There is no love and no peace. If you do not repent and convert your hearts, you will all fall into an abyss.

The messages from the Blessed Mother continued to become even more dire. On August 15, 1982, in front of twenty thousand people, Alphonsine screamed, "I see a river of blood! What does that mean?" Alphonsine described a vision of people killing and cutting each other to pieces and thousands upon thousands of piles of headless corpses.

Some believe that the prophecy of a river of blood was more than a metaphor. It was an accurate prediction of the atrocities of genocide, which came true twelve years later. The *New York Times* reported on May 21, 1994, that as many as ten thousand mutilated bodies from Rwanda's genocide washed down the Kagera River into Lake Victoria in Uganda. Kibeho itself became the site of two massacres. One was in 1994, as people took refuge in the church, and the second was in 1995, with a military-led killing of Hutu refugees.

ANATHALIE'S VISIT TO HEAVEN, PURGATORY, AND HELL

On October 30, 1982, Anathalie took a mystical journey with Mary. The circumstances around the trip were closely observed by a team from the bishop's theological commission. Anathalie's journey began after a five-hour apparition. Her body was examined by the same physicians who had examined Alphonsine, with similar results. Seven hours later, she awoke and was carried to her bed where she did not speak for two days.

She described her journey as seeing vivid colors and light. People traveled by "sliding through the light." The first place they visited was illuminated only by white light. She saw seven angels in white cloaks playing beautiful music without any instruments. Mary called this place "Isangano," a place of communion, and angels praised God, watched over the earth, and assisted humanity when called upon. That was the focal point of her mystical journey.

From there Anathalie and Mary floated to three different worlds. The first world contained millions of people dressed in white. They seemed overwhelmingly happy, but they were not as blissful as the angels. Mary called this place "Isenderezwa z'ibyishimo," the place of the cherished of God.

The second world was in dim light, like dusk. People were dressed in dreary and duller clothes, compared to the other places. Most of the people seemed content, but many seemed sad and even suffering. Mary called this place "Isesengurwa," a place of purification.

The last place was a land of twilight, illuminated only by an unpleasant shade of red. It was dry and hot. She could not look at the people because of their misery and anguish. Anathalie knew it must be hell.

According to Mary:

> Spend two days reflecting in silence on what you have seen. Do not meditate on the angels you saw; they are not of this world. The first place, the happy world of the cherished of God, was reserved for people whose hearts are good, who pray regularly, and who strive always to follow God's will. Our second visit was to the place of purification—for those who called on God only during times of trouble, turning away from him when their troubles were over. The last place of heat had no name and was for those who never paid God any attention at all.

THE FINAL APPARITION IN KIBEHO

The apparitions of Kibeho officially ended on November 28, 1989. Alphonsine, who was at the first apparition, also experienced the Virgin Mary's last apparition. Mary specified that she would not have any more apparitions in Kibeho:

> At this final apparition in Kibeho, the Blessed Mother said, "My children, in truth, I am not staying long as I used to do, as I have told you all that was necessary. I have just told you what more I needed from you. As I said, I wanted to remind you that I am happy. I am happy with the fruits that were born in Rwanda since I came here. Don't worry about the difficulties you have. Nothing is better than having God. My dear children, problems exist everywhere, but the most important thing is to have an accepting heart without complaining. You all who are called crazy because you like to pray, all of you who are called thieves, those to whom they say that you are losing time by giving your life to God, I tell you that one day you will be happy.
>
> "All of you who are sick with incurable diseases, a good heart surpasses all; there are no riches that are beyond a clean heart. All of you who have had difficulties of all kinds, there are difficulties everywhere, in all walks of life. When they don't go away, offer them to God. Every good Christian is requested to offer a sacrifice. All of you who have problems in your families, think of the Holy Family, who lived in poverty, and who lived among those who didn't like them nor understood them, and with the problems you have, come close to them.

> All of you who have dedicated your lives to God, a life like that is not easy. The most important thing is to be faithful to your promises.
>
> "All of you, young people, when you are young, you think that you can do anything; be careful not to fall and damage yourself for good. All of you leaders, who have the capacity to represent many people, don't kill, but save; don't be greedy, but share with others, and don't attempt to hurt those who are trying to expose your wrongdoings. I tell you, anyone you want to hurt, because they love people and are defending human rights, because they are defending the cause of the poor and the simple, because they are trying to defend anything good and trying to love God, I tell you, whatever you do will be in vain.
>
> "My children, saying goodbye to you doesn't mean that I am forgetting Africa, not even the whole world. It doesn't mean that I am going to forget Rwandans. I am asking you not to forget the love I have loved you with, when I came to your country."

The Blessed Mother told the visionaries that suffering is "a part of our daily bread while still on earth." Suffering teaches us things we would not have learned, and it leads to heaven. She said if her warning came to pass, do not cry for those who die. The gates of heaven would be open because they died innocently:

> Cry for those who will remain alive because many will be tempted to violence and revenge. Others will not be able to bear to live with the wrong they have done to others. There will be some who will be left;

> they will be left to tell the goodness of God, because there is nothing else that could console them after the pain they would have experienced.

AUTHENTICATION BY THE CHURCH

An accurate prediction of genocide was a major factor in the local bishop's 2001 decision to declare the 1981 to 1983 visions "worthy of belief." Though more than thirty people claimed to have visions at Kibeho, only three visionaries were authenticated by the bishop.

Two study commissions for authentication were set by the Rwandan bishop in April 1982. One commission consisted of doctors. The second commission consisted of theologians. They reviewed the apparition cases of thirty-three people who claimed to be visionaries.

The commission determined that the three original visionaries—Alphonsine, Anathalie, and Marie-Claire—were worthy of belief. Their visions strengthened the life of faith and prayer. There were no new revelations of church doctrine. They each accurately predicted a future genocide. Their reputations and testimonies were genuine and believable.

Alphonsine reported that Mary told her the last public apparition in Kibeho would occur on November 28, 1989. This date is kept by the ecclesiastical authority as the limit for the occurrence of these apparitions. Many of the other visionaries claimed to have public apparitions beyond that date and could not be supported. None of the remaining thirty people who claimed to be visionaries drew crowds. Some had disquieting personal situations. Others claimed to meet Jesus and were divinely instructed to travel the world to tell their stories. Some of the thirty people seem credible, but based on current evidence, the church cannot authenticate them yet.

CONCLUDING EVENTS

Marie-Claire died during the genocide, and Alphonsine and Anathalie were forced to flee Rwanda. Tens of thousands of pilgrims annually visit the statue of Our Lady of Kibeho in the shrine of Kibeho. Our Lady of Sorrows Basilica is located on the site of a massacre that occurred in Kibeho.

KEY MESSAGES FROM BLESSED MARY

With motherly love and compassion, Mary visits Rwanda before a civil war and genocide begin. Mary requests more prayer from the faithful to help stop or mitigate the war. Mary comes to save souls before it is too late.

Because many atheists do not believe in heaven or hell, Mary takes two visionaries to see heaven, hell, and purgatory. Heaven is reserved for people whose hearts are good, who pray regularly, and who strive to follow God's will. Purgatory is for those who call on God only during times of trouble, turning away from him when their troubles are over. Hell is for those who never pay God any attention at all.

Nothing is better than having God. Suffering teaches things that are not learned otherwise, and it leads to heaven.

CHAPTER 22

1981: Apparition in Medjugorje, Bosnia and Herzegovina

Just as Mary did in Kibeho, Rwanda, she continues her new focus on providing evidence that heaven and hell do exist during her visit to Medjugorje. In Fatima, three visionaries saw visions of hell. In Rwanda, Mary took two visionaries to personally see heaven, purgatory, and hell. In Medjugorje, Mary allowed four additional visionaries to see heaven, purgatory, and hell.

Following the end of World War II, a federation of six independent republics were forged into one country, which was called Yugoslavia. The six republics included Serbia, Croatia, Bosnia-Herzegovina, Montenegro, Slovenia, and Macedonia. The Allies appointed communist dictator Tito to lead the country, and he became Yugoslavia's main unifying force. When Tito died in 1980, political, ethnic, and economic problems began to build within the country.

War broke out in 1991, resulting in the breakup of Yugoslavia by 2001. The Yugoslav wars were most severely felt in Bosnia-Herzegovina because the people there were multiethnic. A history of ethnic cleansing arose once again and brought atrocities to the primary ethnic groups of Muslim, Serb, and Croat. The ethnic groups were primarily divided by religion: Muslims, Orthodox Serbs, and Croatian Catholics. The Bosnian War lasted from 1992 to 1995. In Herzegovina, the majority Croatian Catholics destroyed mosques and Orthodox churches. The war pitted neighbor against neighbor, along ethnic lines, and families and marriages split along ethnic lines as a result of the destruction.

THE APPARITION

Ten years before the ethnic cleansing war would begin, the first apparition in Medjugorje, Bosnia and Herzegovina, occurred on June 24, 1981 around 6:00 p.m. on a hill called Podbrdo. Medjugorje is a town located on the southwestern side of the country of Bosnia and Herzegovina, near Croatia. Six Croatian children, aged from ten to sixteen, were the visionaries, or "seers" of the apparition. For several of the visionaries, now adults, the apparitions continue daily, and for the remaining visionaries, the apparitions occur annually. The apparitions continued during the Yugoslav wars.

In 1981, the six primary seers included sixteen-year-old Mirjana Dragicevic, fifteen-year-old Ivanka Ivankovic, sixteen-year-old Vicka Ivankovic, sixteen-year-old Ivan Dragicevic, sixteen-year-old Marija Pavlovic, and ten-year-old Jakov Colo. None of the children are siblings of each other.

On June 24, the children saw a beautiful woman, bright and shining, with a little child in her arms. The lady did not speak, but she gestured for the children to come closer. However, they were afraid and did not move closer. The lady told them she loved them and vanished.

On June 25, the children met at the same site. There was a flash of light. The beautiful lady appeared, this time without the child, and gestured for them to come closer. They moved closer, fell to their knees, and began to pray the Rosary aloud. The lady joined them in praying the Rosary except when they prayed the "Hail Mary."

On June 26, some of the children's parents advised them to take holy water with them to ensure the apparition was not the devil. Once the apparition appeared, Vicka splashed some holy water toward the lady and said, "If you are our Blessed Mother, please stay, and if you are not, go away from us."

The lady smiled and stayed. When Mirjana asked her name, the lady replied, "I am the Blessed Virgin Mary." On the way back, Mary appeared again to Marija and said, "Peace, peace, and only peace. Peace must reign between people and God, and among all people." Mary spoke to the visionaries in their native language, Croatian.

On June 27, Mary gave a message for the children to pass on to the priests: "May the priests firmly believe and may they take care of the faith of the people." Jakov and Mirjana asked for a sign because people did not believe the children saw Mary and accused them of lying and taking drugs.

Mary replied, "Do not be afraid of anything."

On June 28, a crowd of fifteen thousand people gathered throughout the day to see Mary. The parish priest, Father Jozo Zovko, interviewed the children about their visions. When the children saw Mary, no one else in the audience could see or hear Mary. Vicka asked Mary what she wanted from the children and their priests. Mary replied, "The people should pray and firmly believe. Blessed are those who have not seen and yet believe."

On June 29, the children were examined by a medical doctor and proclaimed healthy. Once in front of Mary, the children asked her to heal a two-year-old boy, Daniel Setka, who was mute and unable to walk.

Mary answered, "Let his parents believe that he will be healed. I cannot heal—only God can. I need your prayers and sacrifices to help me." Later that evening, as the family of the boy was on its way home, they stopped at a restaurant. Miraculously, the child was able to speak and walk. He was completely healed. Word of the miracle boy spread throughout the town.

On June 30, local community officials felt threatened by the crowds and discouraged attendance at the apparition site. The children stayed one kilometer away from their normal meeting place on Podbrdo.

Mary came to them and prayed seven "Our Fathers" with them.

From July 1, 1981 through January 14, 1982, police blocked the children from going to Podbrdo. Mary met them in secret places. When the children asked Mary, at the request of a priest, whether they should pray to Jesus or Mary, she said, "Please pray to Jesus. I am his mother, and I intercede for you with him. But all prayer goes to Jesus. I will help. I will pray, but everything does not depend only on me. It depends also on your strength, the strength of those who pray."

The doubting parish priest let them meet in the church. One day, the priest also saw an apparition of Mary—and he believed. He later testified of his support for the authenticity of the apparitions and was forced to serve a prison sentence.

After January 15, 1982, the children met Mary in a closed portion of the church. In March, the local bishop issued a prohibition on meeting in the church. Beginning in April, the children met Mary in the parish house.

Since 1981, the Blessed Virgin Mary has been giving messages to the world from Medjugorje. Mary says God sent her to earth during a time of grace granted by God:

> I have come to tell the world that God exists. He is the fullness of life, and to enjoy this fullness and peace, you must return to God.

Mary is here to reeducate us and to help us recenter our lives back to God. Her role has always been to guide people to her Son, Jesus.

A VISION OF HEAVEN, PURGATORY, AND HELL

On January 10, 1983, Mirjana was interviewed by Father Tomislav Dragicevic. When asked about her discussions with Mary, Mirjana said she asked questions about heaven, purgatory, and hell that were unclear to her. Mirjana did not understand how a merciful God could throw people into hell to suffer forever. Mary told her that souls who go to hell have ceased thinking favorably about God. They curse him. They opposed God on earth, and they continue their opposition to God in hell. They do not pray in hell. They blame God for everything. They rage against God and suffer, but they always refuse to pray to God.

Mirjana also asked Mary about how many people go to hell. Mary replied that most people go to purgatory, the next greatest number go to hell, and the least number go directly to heaven. People who go directly to heaven are not necessarily people who perform miracles or do great penance; they simply respect their faith and live peacefully—without malice, meanness, or falsehood.

Mirjana saw a vision of heaven during an apparition and described it in a separate interview:

> I saw heaven as if it were a movie. The first thing I noticed was the faces of the people there; they were radiating a type of inner light which showed how immensely happy they were. The trees, the meadows, the sky are totally different from anything we know on the earth. And the light is much more brilliant. Heaven is beautiful beyond any possible comparison with anything I know of on the earth.

When asked if people in heaven have bodies, Mirjana answered, "Yes." They also asked her what ages they were:

> They were different from what we are like now. Perhaps they were all around thirty years of age … They were walking in a beautiful park. They have everything. They need or want nothing. They are

> totally full ... They were dressed in the types of clothing that Jesus wore.

During another interview, Mirjana was asked about purgatory:

> There are several levels in purgatory. The more you pray on earth, the higher your level in purgatory will be ... The lowest level is the closest to hell, where the suffering is the most intense. The highest level is closest to heaven, and there the suffering is the least. What level you are on depends on the state of purity of your soul. The lower the level the people are on in purgatory, the less they are able to pray and the more they suffer. The higher the level a person is in purgatory, the easier it is for him to pray, the more he enjoys praying and the less he suffers ... The Blessed Mother has asked us to pray for the souls in purgatory. They are helpless to pray for themselves. Through prayer, we on earth can do much to help them. The Blessed Mother told me that when souls leave purgatory and go to heaven most go on Christmas Day.

> Many people were there. They were suffering immensely ... They were normal people, all kinds. There was much physical suffering ... I could see the people shivering, thrashing, and writhing in pain ... I saw this place for a short time ... The Blessed Mother was with me (during the vision). She explained to me that she wanted me to see purgatory. She said so many people on earth today do not even know about purgatory ... I could not hear them. I only saw them. The Blessed Mother said so many people who die are quite abandoned

by their loved ones. They cannot help themselves in purgatory. They are totally dependent on the prayers and sacrifices of the generous people on earth who remember them. Our Blessed Mother hopes her own children will help the souls in purgatory by prayer and fasting and various penance for the poor souls to make restitution for them … Those who have died no longer have free will as they had on earth. They no longer have a body. It is no longer possible for them to make up for the things that they did when they had their body that hurt and harmed themselves and others.

On July 24, 1982, the Blessed Mother said, "We go to heaven in full consciousness of the separation of the body and soul. It is false to teach people that we are reborn many times and that we pass to different bodies. One is born only once. The body, drawn from the earth, decomposes after death. It never comes back to life again. Humans receive a transfigured body. Whoever has done very much evil during his life can go straight to heaven if he confesses, is truly sorry for what he has done, and receives Communion at the end of his life." Our Lady said that the souls in purgatory can see their loved ones during those moments when we pray for them by name.

Marija described purgatory in several interviews:

Purgatory is a large place. It is foggy. It is ash gray. It is misty. You cannot see people there. It is as if they are immersed in deep clouds. You can feel that the people in the mist are traveling, hitting each

> other. They can pray for us but not for themselves. They are desperately in need of our prayers. The Blessed Mother asks us to pray for the poor souls in purgatory, because during their life here, one moment they thought there was no God, then they recognized Him, then they went to purgatory where they saw there is a God, and now they need our prayers. With our prayers we can send them to heaven. The biggest suffering that souls in purgatory have is that they see there is a God, but they did not accept him here on earth. Now they long so much to come close to God. Now they suffer so intensely, because they recognize how much they have hurt God, how many chances they had on earth, and how many times they disregarded God.

Mirjana wondered about different religions on earth and asked Mary about it. The Madonna always stresses that there is but one God, and that people have enforced unnatural separation between religions, like Serbian Orthodox and Muslims. Every religion should be respected. Mary deplored the lack of religious unity.

OTHER RELIGIONS

In February 1983, Ivanka was interviewed by Father Svetozar Kraljevic. Ivanka asked Mary about different religions. The Madonna told her that religions are separated on earth, but the people of all religions are accepted by her Son. That does not mean everyone goes to heaven. That depends on what each person deserves.

Marija was also interviewed about heaven, purgatory, and hell. Mary showed her visions of all three places. She said that when a man dies, God gives him special graces and blessings to decide where he should go himself. God gives him a scene, reviewing his whole life. Once he fully understands, he will answer truthfully.

Marija said that once a soul is in purgatory, the soul can only go to heaven:

> We choose heaven, hell, or purgatory for ourselves. The Blessed Mother explained to me that at death we are the same person we are in life, though we no longer have the use of our body. It returns to the earth. We receive the light at death to see the plan God has had for us from the beginning. We then understand how we have chosen to comply with his divine plan. In the light of truth, we know where we belong, where we fit, and we choose heaven, hell, or purgatory.

A VISIT TO HEAVEN, PURGATORY, AND HELL

On November 2, 1981, while the visionaries were children, Mary took Vicka and Jakov with her to visit heaven, purgatory, and hell. Jakov and Vicka are the only two human beings in the history of the world who were physically in body, taken by the hand by the Holy Virgin Mary, to heaven, purgatory, and hell. Our Lady wanted to dispel atheistic thoughts that these places are not real. They absolutely do exist.

In an interview about heaven, Vicka explained that when they arrived at heaven, there was a great big wooden door. She said that the door was closed, but when they arrived, Our Lady opened it, and they entered heaven. She said St. Peter was standing inside just to the right of the door:

> Heaven is a vast space, and it has a brilliant light which does not leave it. It is a life which we do not know here on earth. We saw people dressed in gray, pink, and yellow robes. They were walking, praying, and singing. Small angels were flying

> above them. The Blessed Mother showed us how happy these people are. You can see it on their faces. But it is impossible to describe with words the great happiness I saw in heaven ... In paradise, when the Blessed Mother passed, everybody responded to her, and she to them. There was a recognition between them ... They were standing there communicating with her, like in a tunnel, only it wasn't exactly like a tunnel, but a tunnel is the closest comparison. People were praying, they were singing, they were looking ... People in heaven know the absolute fullness of a created being.

Vicka and Jakov learned from Mary how much souls in purgatory depend on prayers from people on earth. The responsibility of praying for the souls in purgatory weighed heavily on their hearts.

In interviews, Vicka described purgatory:

> Purgatory is an endless space of ashy color. It was quite dark. I could feel people strangling and suffering there. The Blessed Mother told us we should be praying for souls stranded in purgatory. She said only our prayers and sacrifices can release them from that place ... The people there are helpless. They are really suffering. We can be like Jesus a little bit if we just do some voluntary penance for the souls in purgatory, especially for the ones who are abandoned by their families on earth ... I am aware of their suffering. I know some of their torment. I know how desperately they need our prayers. They are so lonely that it is almost sickening to remember those moments I was there. It is really a great joy to do penance for the poor souls because I know how much it helps them ...

> And many of our family members who have died desperately need our prayers. The Blessed Mother says we must pray courageously for them so that they might go to heaven. They are powerless to help themselves.

Ivan only spoke a little about heaven, hell, and purgatory:

> The Blessed Mother told me that those who go to purgatory are those who prayed and believed only occasionally—that they were filled with doubt, that they were not certain that God exists. They did not know how to pray while on earth, or if they did know how, they did not pray … Souls in purgatory suffer. If no one prays for them, they suffer even more.

ALL SOULS DAY

Catholics celebrate All Souls Day each year on November 2. It's a specific day reserved to pray for the dead in purgatory. Mary took Vicka and Jakov to purgatory on All Souls Day.

Orthodox Christians reserve the Saturday before Pentecost each year to pray for those in purgatory. They also pray for souls in purgatory on six other days during the year. The specific days vary based on the type of Orthodox Church.

SUFFERING FOR THOSE IN PURGATORY

When Vicka saw how some souls in purgatory were abandoned with no one on earth to pray for them, she felt great compassion and asked how she could help.

Mary asked that she first discuss it with her spiritual advisor. Once Mary was convinced Vicka completely understood the seriousness of her request, it was approved. Unfortunately, Vicka was afflicted with a brain tumor that caused painful headaches and high fevers, which would cause her to frequently fall into a coma. She suffered from this affliction for several years.

In January 1988, Mary told Vicka her suffering would end later that year, on September 25, and to tell no one. Vicka recorded the date on a paper, placed it in a sealed envelope, and gave it to a Catholic commission investigating the apparitions. They were instructed not to open the envelope until told. On September 25, Vicka's symptoms disappeared and never returned. After the commission was given permission to open the envelope, they read the words of Mary foretelling of Vicka's healing and recovery.

MORE ABOUT HELL

When asked about hell, Vicka said,

> We saw many people in hell. Many are there already, and many more will go there when they die … The Blessed Mother says that those people who are in hell are there because they chose to go there. They wanted to go to hell … We all know that there are persons on this earth who simply do not admit that God exists, even though he helps them, gives them life and sun and rain and food. He always tries to nudge them onto the path of holiness. They just say they do not believe, and they deny him. They deny him, even when it is time to die. And they continue to deny him, after they are dead. It is their choice. It is their will that they go to hell. They choose hell.
>
> In the center of this place is a great fire, like an ocean of raging flames. We could see people before they went into the fire, and then we could see them coming out of the fire. Before they go into the fire, they look like normal people. The more they are

> against God's will, the deeper they enter the fire, and the deeper they go, the more they rage against him. When they come out of the fire, they do not have human shape anymore; they are more like grotesque animals, but unlike anything on earth. They look as if they were never human beings before … They were horrible, ugly, angry. And each was different; no two looked alike … When they came out, they were raging and smashing everything around and hissing and gnashing and screeching.
>
> People turn away from God by choices they make. In this way they choose to enter the fire of hell where they burn away all connection to God. That is why they can never get back to God. It takes God's mercy to get back to him. In hell, they no longer have access to God's mercy … They choose to destroy their beauty and goodness. They choose to be ugly and horrible. People do this all the time. Each choice that is against God, God's Commandments, God's will, singes God's image in us … They become one with hell even while they have their body. At death they go on as they were when they had a body.

A MESSAGE OF PEACE

During an interview, Ivan was asked which message was most important. After thinking, Ivan said, "Peace, you must have peace within your own heart first. Be at peace with yourself."

> If you have peace in your own heart, you can then have peace with God. Once you are at peace with God, you can be at peace with others.

Overall, the Medjugorje apparitions contained a message of peace for the world. Mary also made a call to conversion, prayer, and fasting. According to their ability to understand, each individual visionary received shared secrets about future events from Mary. A total of ten secrets were told to each visionary. Some of the secrets would pertain to the whole world. Others would concern only the visionaries themselves or the town where they lived.

OVERWHELMING LOVE

On December 3, 1988, Marija experienced her daily apparition with Mary: "Dear children, I give you my love, so you can give it to others." During that time, Marija felt overwhelming love from the Blessed Mother. Marija was known for being especially warm and loving to others.

REVEALING THE THIRD OF TEN SECRETS

Thus far, only one secret has been announced publicly. The third secret was revealed to the visionaries while they were still children. In Mary's third secret, she promised to leave a supernatural, indestructible, and visible sign on Podbrdo, now called Apparition Hill, in Medjugorje, where she first appeared:

> This sign will be given for atheists. You faithful already have signs and you have become the sign for atheists. You faithful must not wait for the sign before you convert; convert soon. This time is a time of grace for you. You can never thank God enough for his grace. The time is for deepening your faith, and for your conversion. When the sign comes, it will be too late for many.

Three warnings will be given to the world in the form of events on earth. The appearance of an indestructible sign will be the third event. Three days before each event, Father Petar Liubicic, who was selected by Mirjana, will publicly and officially announce each of the three impending events. After the first event, the other two events will occur in a short period of time. The period between the first and second event will be a period of great grace and conversion. According to Mirjana, who was born in 1965, the predicted events will occur during her lifetime and are near. Father Liubicic, who will announce the events, was born in 1946.

ILLUMINATION OF CONSCIENCE

Mary also spoke about three events, including a supernatural sign, when she appeared in apparitions in Garabandal, Spain, beginning in 1961. Authentication by the Catholic Church of the Garabandal apparitions has not yet been determined and remains under review. However, the Garabandal message about the three events is the same as the third secret in Medjugorje—with one exception. In Garabandal, Mary shared additional details about the first and second events.

The first event is an illumination of conscience for every individual simultaneously. It will be seen and felt interiorly by each person in the world, including atheists and people of all religions. Everyone will know it is from God and that God is real. In an illumination of conscience, people will see the wrong they have done and the good they have failed to do. They will see themselves as God sees them. It is meant to purify people and correct the conscience of the world. This will be a time of divine mercy. Many will convert and confess their sins. Some individuals may die from being horrified at seeing themselves through the eyes of God. Some atheists will convert, but others will continue to hate God.

The second event involves healing miracles. The third event will be the supernatural sign for remaining atheists.

WORLD CHASTISEMENT

The ninth and tenth secrets are genuinely concerning and troubling. There will be punishment and chastisement for the sins of the world because we cannot expect the entire world to be converted. However, the punishment can be diminished by prayer and penance. Mirjana says that one of the evils that threatened the world, the one contained in the seventh secret, has already been averted through prayer and fasting. Mirjana tells us not to forget that—through prayer and fasting—wars can be avoided and natural laws can be suspended.

SATAN'S HUNDRED-YEAR TRIAL

Blessed Mary talked to Mirjana and said,

> Excuse me for this, but you must realize Satan exists. One day he appeared before the throne of God and asked permission to submit the church to a period of trial. God gave him permission to try the church for one century, with extended powers. Satan chose the twentieth century. This century is under the power of the devil; but when the secrets confided to you come to pass, his power will be destroyed. Even now he is beginning to lose his power and has become aggressive. He is destroying marriages, causing abortions, creating divisions among priests and is responsible for obsessions and murder. You must protect yourselves against these things through fasting and prayer, especially community prayer. Carry blessed objects with you. Put them in your house, and restore the use of holy water.

The century of Satan testing the church is consistent with a reported apocalyptic vision seen by a previous Catholic pope. After celebrating Mass on October 13, 1884, Pope Leo XIII saw a vision of the future of the church and collapsed. After being helped to his feet, the pope told of a vision of Satan approaching the throne of God, bragging that he could destroy God's church. God reminded Satan that his church could never be destroyed. Satan replied, "Grant me one century and more power for those who will serve me, and I will destroy it." God granted him one hundred years. The Lord then revealed twentieth-century events to Pope Leo XIII. He saw wars, immorality, genocide, and apostacy in the world on a large scale.

VATICAN AUTHENTICATION CONTROVERSY

Medjugorje is a controversial Marian apparition site for potential Vatican authentication. On April 11, 1991, a commission of Yugoslavian bishops declared, "On the basis of the investigations thus far, it cannot be affirmed that one is dealing with supernatural apparitions and revelations." They did recognize, however, that believers and nonbelievers were visiting Medjugorje in great numbers and converting to a more faithful Christian life, which required attention and pastoral care. In this declaration, the commission investigating Medjugorje was not hindering anyone or anything connected with it.

Pope John Paul II repeatedly encouraged the bishops who came to him about Medjugorje to go there—and to allow the faithful to go there as well. Hundreds of cardinals and bishops from around the world went to Medjugorje and came away impressed. In October 1994, Pope John Paul II said, "Authorize everything that concerns Medjugorje."

In 2010, Pope Benedict XVI formed a second commission of international bishops to study Medjugorje for potential authentication. Upon completion, the final report was given to Pope Francis. Speaking informally, Francis said he has grave doubts about the apparitions' authenticity while the visionaries are adults. He is also concerned about Mary's portrayal as a "telegraph office" with monthly messages for the world. The commission report recommends the early apparitions be declared authentic and supernatural. The apparitions that occurred when the visionaries were adults require more investigation.

In May 2019, Pope Francis approved pilgrimages to Medjugorje organized by dioceses and parishes. They no longer had to be organized only by private companies. No final decision from the Vatican on the authenticity of the visions has been made. Pope Francis assigned an archbishop to review the pastoral aspects of Medjugorje.

The Vatican typically does not authenticate apparitions while they are ongoing. Visionaries could then misuse their authority once they are deemed authentic by contradicting the deposit of faith, the body of revealed truth in the scriptures, and tradition proposed by the Roman Catholic Church for the belief of the faithful in new apparitions. The Marian apparitions at Medjugorje are quite different than most other apparitions. These apparitions have occurred with the same visionaries over decades. It seems Mary plans to continue the apparitions with these visionaries through most of their lives, although appearing less often. The visions typically end within one year at most of the other Marian apparition sites.

[With one exception, everything in this book concerning the Medjugorje apparitions is from the visionaries when they were children, which may be authenticated by the Vatican in the future. This includes information on heaven, purgatory, and hell. It also includes the third secret, a permanent sign. The one exception is the following section, "Mary's Continuing Messages." This is controversial because these apparition messages came when the visionaries were adults, and they may never be authenticated by the Vatican.]

MARY'S CONTINUING MESSAGES

Mary leaves a public message in Medjugorje at least once each month. Some of her past monthly messages are as follows:

> Dear children, this is the reason for my presence among you for such a long time: to lead you on the path to Jesus. I want to save you and, through you, to save the whole world. Many people now live without faith; some do not even want to hear about Jesus, but they still want peace and satisfaction. Children, here is the reason I need your prayer: prayer is the only way to save humanity.
>
> Children, darkness reigns over the whole world. People are attracted by many things and they forget about the more important.
>
> Light won't reign in the world until people accept Jesus, until they live his words, which is the Word of the Gospel.
>
> Dear children, by the act of the decision and love of God, I am chosen to be the mother of God and your mother. But, also by my will and my immeasurable love for the Heavenly Father and my complete trust in him, my body was the chalice of the God-man. I was in the service of truth, love and salvation, as I am now among you to call you, my children, apostles of my love, to be carriers of truth; to call you to spread his words, the words of salvation, by your will and love for my Son: that with your actions you may show, to all those who have not come to know my Son, his love. You will find strength in the Eucharist—my Son who feeds you

> with his body and strengthens you with his blood. My children, fold your hands and look at the cross in silence. In this way, you are drawing faith to be able to transmit it; you are drawing truth to be able to discern; you are drawing love that you may know to love truly. My children, apostles of my love, fold your hands, look at the cross. Only in the cross is salvation. Thank you.

SUPERNATURAL PHENOMENA

There is a fourteen-ton cement cross on Cross Mountain in Medjugorje. In August 1981, the Croatian word "Mir" which means "peace," was written in the sky at night above the large cross. Many people from the village, including the parish priest, saw it. On other days, the cross was seen to spin or disappear altogether. Occasionally, a silhouette of Our Lady was observed at the foot of the cross at night.

In Medjugorje, the sun has frequently been observed moving in miraculous ways. It would pulsate, spin, show a rainbow of colors, and change into a white disc. Brightly colored ribbons appeared around the sun. The sun appeared to dance. They were miracles of the sun.

During an adoration service, a Mass held solely in adoration of God, a bright light appeared just above the monstrance. A monstrance holds a large Communion wafer, which becomes the body of Christ after consecration by a priest. When in the presence of consecrated Communion bread, Catholics believe they are in the presence of Christ. Immediately following the adoration service, the figure of a heart appeared.

Many visitors to Medjugorje reported that their rosaries turned to a gold color. When they pull them out to pray the Rosary, the silver chain turns golden. Some believe it's a gift from God for making the pilgrimage. Others believe it's a sign of prayers answered.

Blessed Mary said these supernatural signs are intended to validate the authenticity of the apparitions and highlight the urgency of her message.

PILGRIMAGE SITE

Since the apparitions began in 1981, more than forty million people of all faiths, from all over the world, have visited Medjugorje. Currently, about one million people visit there each year. They leave with spiritual strengthening and renewal. Millions of spiritual conversions have occurred. There were many miracle healings of body, mind, and spirit.

An eighty-five-year-old man was blind due to a stroke. His wife gathered some plants from Apparition Hill and placed them in a water vase to let them soak. Then the elderly man washed with the water from the vase and was immediately able to see.

Two women in wheelchairs, due to having multiple sclerosis for twenty-five years, read about Medjugorje and prayed for healing. They were healed instantaneously and could walk. The mother of a six-month-old baby covered in eczema gathered some herbs at Medjugorje and put them in water. She washed her baby with the water. The baby was healed. Many other healings were reported by people who used soil, flowers, or herbs from Apparition Hill and mixed them with water to apply to an afflicted area of their bodies. They were healed from blindness, deafness, paralysis, and other diseases.

CONCLUDING EVENTS

Today, all six of the Medjugorje visionaries are married with children. While many of them considered full-time service to Christ as nuns or priests, they each concluded it would be better to help Mary communicate her messages in Medjugorje without the limitations imposed by having other significant responsibilities. Five of the six visionaries stated they would be alive when the permanent sign comes. They were born in the 1960s. The youngest visionary, Jakov, says only that the timing is a secret.

Medjugorje's message is one of love and peace. It is a call for atheists and agnostics to believe in God. It is a call for believers to pray more and become closer to God. The mother of Jesus Christ is making this little village a mouthpiece for her Son's message to the world. His message sanctifies all faiths that have God as their foundation of belief. It can be understood and accepted by Catholic, Orthodox, Protestant, Muslim, or Jew, and it is meant for all of them. Medjugorje is the new birthplace of tremendous renewal in the ways of God for a troubled world.

KEY MESSAGES FROM MARY

Mary comes to Medjugorje to request more prayer from the faithful and to tell the world God exists. Mary gives love so it can be shared with others. She clarifies that all prayer goes to Jesus or his Father and only God can perform healing miracles.

Heaven is for people who respect their faith and live peacefully and without malice. Mary's Son accepts all religions in heaven, but each person must still believe in God and deserve a place in heaven. Heaven has brilliant light. People have indescribable happiness. They have transfigured bodies, not their earthly ones. They all look to be about thirty years old.

Hell is for people who oppose God and refuse to believe in God. Hell has a great fire in the center. People look like humans and then go into the fire. They come out raging, no longer in human form, and look like grotesque animals.

Purgatory is for those who pray and believe only occasionally, are filled with doubt, and are not certain God exists. Purgatory contains different levels depending on the purity of the soul. There is more suffering and difficulty praying for those on the lower levels of purgatory. However, on the higher levels, there is less suffering and it is easier to pray. For those who suffer in purgatory, only prayer and sacrifice from people on earth can release them to heaven. Those in purgatory can pray, but they cannot pray for themselves. When souls leave purgatory and go to heaven, most go on Christmas Day. Souls in purgatory can see loved ones on earth momentarily when they are remembered in prayer by name. It encourages them to see family gatherings.

Most people go to purgatory; the second most go to hell; the least number go directly to heaven.

There will soon be three events beginning with an illumination of conscience for each person in the world. Individuals will see themselves as God sees them – the wrong they have done and the good they failed to do. God will perform healing miracles in the second event and then leave a supernatural, indestructible, and visible sign on Apparition Hill in Medjugorje for atheists. Now is the time for the faithful to deepen their faith and pray for the conversion of nonbelievers. When the sign comes, it will be too late for many. These events will occur during the visionaries' lifetimes (they were born in the 1960s).

Three days before each event, Father Petar Liubicic, who was born in 1946, will publicly announce the impending event. These events will occur in a short period of time. The period between the first and second events will be a period of great grace and conversion. The predicted events are near.

There will be punishment and chastisement for the sins of the world because we cannot expect the entire world to be converted. However, the punishment can be diminished by prayer and penance. Through prayer and fasting, wars can be avoided—and natural laws can be suspended. Mary calls for atheists and agnostics to passionately believe in God.

CHAPTER 23
1983: Apparition in San Nicolas, Argentina

Mary has visited daily with the six visionaries in Medjugorje, beginning in 1981, and continuing today. In 1983, Mary also started visiting with a visionary in Argentina. Mary's apparitions at both locations continue today.

San Nicolas is a city of 138,000 people and is located 150 miles northwest of Buenos Aires, Argentina. On September 25, 1983, in San Nicolas, Gladys Quiroga de Motta noticed her rosary beads were glowing like molten steel. She ran to get her neighbors to come and see. They saw it and told others. Soon, groups of people in town were praying the Rosary daily. Rosaries in other homes throughout San Nicolas also began to glow without explanation.

Gladys was a forty-six-year-old wife and mother of two daughters. She was also a grandmother. With only a fourth-grade education, she had little knowledge of the Bible or theology.

APPARITIONS AND MESSAGES

One night, as Gladys knelt alone in her bedroom to pray, she looked up and saw the Blessed Virgin in front of her. Mary was radiating light. She wore a blue gown with a veil and held the baby Jesus and a large rosary in her arms. Mary smiled, but she did not speak—and then she vanished.

On October 7, 1983, Gladys saw Mary again. Gladys saw five apparitions of Mary in silence. On October 13, 1983, during the sixth apparition, Mary finally said, "You have been faithful. Do not be afraid."

One month after the first apparition, Mary gave Gladys a white rosary and said, "Receive this rosary from my hands and keep it forever and ever. You are obedient. I am happy because of it. Rejoice, for God is with you."

By mid-November, the apparitions were happening every day. Mary requested a church be built. On November 24, Gladys walked to the location where Mary wanted the church. She saw a powerful shaft of light coming down from the heavens and marking the site for a new church.

Mary asked Gladys to look for a statue that had been blessed by a pope and forgotten in a church. On November 27, 1983, Gladys found the statue in the belfry of the cathedral. The statue was the mother of God holding the child Jesus. Pope Leo XIII had blessed it in Rome. The statue resembled the apparition.

Gladys recorded Mary's messages in writing after each apparition:

> All humanity is contaminated. It does not know what it wants, and it is the evil one's chance, but he will not be the winner. Christ Jesus will win the great battle, my daughter. You must not let yourselves be surprised. You must be alert. For this reason, daughter, I ask for so much prayer, so much obedience to God. I say this for the whole world. (December 27, 1983)

> Those who offended Christ Jesus are like those who scourged him and crucified him. That is how he feels it. He suffers offenses and injustices so

intensely. Remember that the God who gives life is the same one who will comfort your sorrow and will grant you the joy of life everlasting. Amen, Amen. (June 18, 1984)

What value prayer has for the Lord, you cannot imagine! My children, that is why I ask for so much prayer! Say the Holy Rosary meditating! I assure you that your prayers will rise like a true song of love to the Lord. (June 13, 1985)

Daughter, the Prince of Evil pours out his venom today with all his might, because he sees that his sorry reign is ending; little is left to him. His end is near. Amen, Amen. (March 7, 1986)

My daughter, the evil one is triumphant now, it is true, but it is a victory that will last briefly. The Lord is only giving him time, the same time that he gives humanity to return to God. (October 11, 1986)

STIGMATA

Gladys received more than 1,800 messages from the Virgin Mary. She also received sixty-eight apparitions and messages from Jesus. In 1984, Gladys received the wounds of stigmata on her hands, feet, side, and shoulder, which are the six wounds of Christ.

Genuine stigmata wounds are distinct from other wounds arising from pathology. Stigmata wounds are located where the crucified Christ's six wounds were located: on his side, hands, feet, and shoulder. Pathological wounds are more randomly located. Genuine stigmata wounds bleed more heavily on Good Fridays. Pathological wounds do not. Blood flow from stigmata wounds does not harm the individual and cannot be treated with medication. The wounds never close or worsen. A sweet odor emanates from the wounds instead of the smell of blood.

MIRACLES

There were several documented miracle healings related to the apparitions. The first miracle occurred in 1984. A seven-year-old boy, Gonzalo Miguel, was healed of a terminal brain tumor.

MESSAGES FROM MARY AND JESUS

In one message, Mary said, "Many hearts do not accept my invitation to prayer and to conversion. That is why the work of the devil is growing and expanding." She warns, humanity is "in the process of falling into a progressive self-destruction. It is up to you to set your eyes and your heart on God. I want to cure my children from this illness which is materialism; an illness which makes many suffer. I want to help them discover Christ, and I want to make it known to them that Christ prevails over everything." She stressed the importance of prayer, especially the Rosary.

In 1987, Gladys reported seeing separate apparitions of Mary and Jesus. Gladys communicated a warning for humanity and new expectations.

> If this generation will not listen to the mother of Jesus, it will perish. Everyone is asked to listen to her. Conversion is necessary. The world is warned their souls are in danger. Many are lost. Few will find salvation unless they accept Jesus as their Savior. The mother of Jesus must be accepted. She must be heard in the totality of her messages. The world must discover the richness she brings to Christians. The children of sin will grow up in sin if their unbelief increases. There needs to be a

renewal of the spirit, a detachment from death, and an attachment to life. Jesus chose the heart of his mother, so that what he asks will be achieved. Souls will come to Jesus through the means of Mary's Immaculate Heart.

CONCLUDING EVENTS

Gladys was always available to the church and shared all the messages. She continues to live a life of devotion and keeps a low profile.

Bishop Castagna ordered the construction of a shrine, as Mary requested, and work began in 1987. The shrine was consecrated in 1990. An investigation of the apparitions by a commission of theologians and doctors was completed. On May 22, 2016, Bishop Cardelli approved the apparitions from 1983 to 1990 as "worthy of belief." The bishop approved publication and broad dissemination of the messages of Our Lady of the Rosary in San Nicolas.

CONTROVERSY

However, the apparitions and messages continued for Gladys beyond 1990. It is very unusual for the Catholic Church to approve apparitions while they are ongoing. In this case, they did so, with a cutoff date of 1990. All apparitions and messages from 1983 through 1990 are considered authentic messages. After 1990, it seems Gladys may have occasionally confused her own reflections with Mary's messages. The Catholic Church states that the 1990 cutoff date does not mean the apparitions have suddenly been deemed untrue. As a matter of fact, the church stands behind the ongoing apparitions and messages beyond 1990. They choose to wait and follow their process of using a new commission to evaluate the latest apparitions (beyond 1990) at some future time. They also stopped publication of the new messages.

NEW CHURCH AND STATUE

In 2008, a magnificent new church was completed in honor of the twenty-fifth anniversary of the first apparition. A dedication of the church and a new wooden statue of Our Lady of the Rosary was attended by two hundred thousand people. On the twenty-fifth day of each month, the bishop leads a processional often accompanied by a hundred thousand people.

KEY MESSAGES FROM BLESSED MARY

Mary visits Argentina to request more prayers from the faithful. She warns the work of Satan is growing. However, Christ will prevail over him. Mary calls for the conversion of sinners.

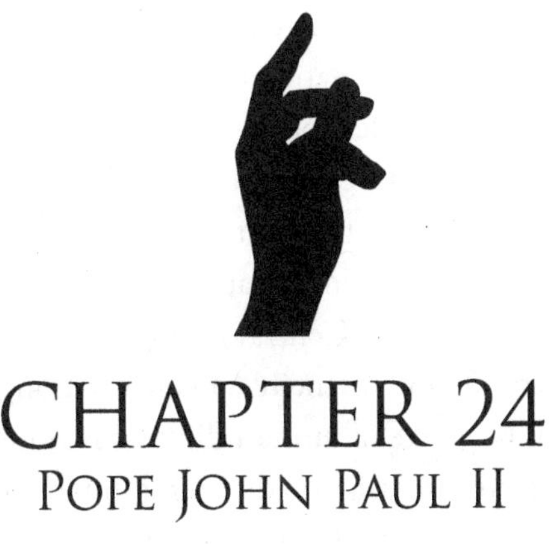

CHAPTER 24
POPE JOHN PAUL II

Pope John Paul II was born in Poland in 1920 and named Karol Wojtyla. He was raised by pious parents. Due to illnesses, his family suffered many setbacks. Shortly before Karol's birth, his sister died. When Karol was eight years old, his mother passed away. At age twelve, his older brother died. When his father died eight years later, Karol found himself alone in the world at age twenty.

Karol studied to become a priest and rose through Catholic leadership ranks to become cardinal of Krakow. Upon election to the papacy, John Paul II was the first non-Italian in modern history to be chosen as leader of the worldwide Roman Catholic Church. He served as pope for 1.2 billion Catholics from 1978 until his death in 2005.

ACCOMPLISHMENTS

As pope, John Paul traveled to 129 countries and spoke eight languages fluently. By placing his focus outside of the Vatican, he became a social influencer across the world. He was appreciated by Catholics, Protestants, Orthodox Christians, and people of other religions. John Paul rekindled the faith of Catholic youth across the globe by starting World Youth Day. Every three years, millions of Catholic youth travel to one city in the world to celebrate their religion together in an international setting.

Pope John Paul II understood his role in combatting the spread of communist atheism. His early years in communist Poland and his devotion to Mary revealed the immense damage to humanity that was perpetrated by Russia. John Paul used his global reputation to help topple communism in Central Europe.

He was careful not to incite violence among the masses of people. Instead, he spoke of human dignity, religious freedom, and the triumph of culture and truth over human political systems. Just as Mary requested in Fatima, John Paul encouraged prayer and inspired hope. His success with the peaceful fall of Soviet communism started a slow reversal of atheism in Central Europe, as well as Russia and the former Soviet republics.

John Paul's best friend was a Jewish man from his hometown in Poland. This friend was also the first person to officially visit John Paul after his election to pope. When they were younger, they both experienced the horrors of the Holocaust. Despite having different religious views, they formed a bond of friendship that lasted their entire lives.

During his papacy, John Paul helped heal relations with other major religions in the world. He embraced the "Fundamental Agreement" between the Vatican and Israel, which governs property rights of Catholic holy sites in Israel. He respectfully visited non-Catholic holy sites of the Judaic, Islamic, and Eastern Orthodox religions.

Pope John Paul II canonized more saints than all the popes over the previous five hundred years combined, dating back to the Protestant Reformation. He changed the Vatican canonization process to approve saints in a shorter time frame. Hundreds of contemporaries now serve as examples of how to live a holy life. Two miracles are required to be associated with each saint prior to their final canonization. John Paul knew that showcasing modern miracles and saints would save more souls.

INFLUENCED BY MARY

Historians are quick to recognize all these outward accomplishments of Pope John Paul II. However, the key to his success may have come from his personal devotion to the Blessed Virgin Mary. John Paul was a fervent admirer of Mary. He visited many of the Marian apparition sites throughout the world.

John Paul listened carefully to Mary's messages and understood her foremost goal was to save souls. Mary used miracles by God at her apparition sites to achieve her goal. By visiting Mary's holy apparition sites, John Paul brought international attention to the healing miracles of Jesus. Many souls were saved as a result of John Paul's devotion to Mary.

John Paul's strategic decisions were guided by prayer with God and understanding messages from Mary. He spent many hours on his knees in prayer in the private chapel in his Vatican apartment. Each day, John Paul would pray at dawn and again in the evening after dinner. He was seen flat on his stomach on the chapel floor, with arms outstretched, in prayer.

John Paul's success against communist atheism was a direct result of Mary's messages in Fatima. After the failed assassination attempt against him, John Paul read Mary's third secret. That led to his public consecration of the entire world to the Immaculate Heart of Mary. The Soviet Union collapsed seven years later. Through prayer alone, the Holy Spirit peacefully ended forced atheism for 340 million people in twenty-two countries.

A MAN OF GOD

Pope John Paul II was truly a man of God. He was filled with the Holy Spirit. Other world religious leaders could sense it when they were near him. John Paul did not focus on the popular political topics of the day. He did not spend his time on people's differences. Instead, John Paul focused on Christ's mission of saving souls. In the process of saving souls, John Paul achieved many other accomplishments.

On the day Pope John Paul II died, thousands of people came to St. Peter's Square and held a spontaneous vigil during John Paul's final hours of life. The presence of both Protestants and Catholics from all over the world was evidence of their mutual respect. John Paul emerged as a leader for all of Christianity when it was needed to rid the world of communist atheism from Russia. His leadership was rare and is certainly missed.

CHAPTER 25

MARY'S DIRE WARNING FOR THE TWENTY-FIRST CENTURY

At every apparition site, Mary asks the faithful to pray more. More prayer brings them closer to her Son, Jesus. More prayer saves souls from going to hell. Prayer for those in purgatory helps them advance toward heaven. Prayer can heal the sick. Prayer can avoid plagues and famine. Prayer can mitigate or avoid war altogether. Prayer can conquer atheistic governments without war. Mary requests more prayer.

During the twentieth century, atheism made itself firmly at home in this world. Denial of God was widespread in the ideologies, plans, and politics of human beings. For this reason, Mary's evangelical call for prayer by the faithful for atheist repentance and conversion was more relevant than ever.

AN INCREASE IN THE NUMBER AND LENGTH OF MESSAGES

In the sixteenth and seventeenth centuries, Mary limits her appearances on earth to a small number of visionaries. During those apparitions, she chooses to remain silent and communicate messages through gestures, feelings of peace and love, and miracles.

During the nineteenth century, Mary visits earth more often. She speaks directly to some visionaries using an economy of words.

Mary greatly increases her visits to earth in the twentieth century. She even returns to the same visionaries thousands of times. Mary visits one apparition site every day for several decades. She also speaks at length with multiple visionaries together and openly answers their questions. She allows some visionaries to personally see heaven, purgatory, and hell. We learn the most from Mary during the twentieth century.

Through the centuries, industrial revolution and advances in technology increased the capability of war in the world. The new capabilities incented more dictators to wage warfare with higher levels of devastation. During the past century, Satan was given more power to turn people away from God. Together, these developments culminated in the highest levels of brutality ever experienced on earth.

The increase in human inhumanity to other humans created a need for more divine intervention in the world. Mary recognized the need, visited more often, and stayed longer. Mary's communications seem to increase with a rise in the risk of many spending eternity in hell.

ATHEISM

Mary warns the world of the immense damage to humanity that is perpetrated by atheist governments. She asks the faithful for more prayer and reparations for the sins of others. Mary requests prayer to support her efforts to bring peace to all nations, especially those with atheist governments and those that oppress religion.

There are more than a billion people in the world today who describe themselves as religiously unaffiliated. Many of them are in areas under current or former atheist governments, including China, North Korea, Russia, former Soviet republics, and Central

Europe. However, they also include a growing number of atheists and agnostics in every country throughout the world.

In 1951, Mary predicted China would return to "Mother church" after much fighting. The outcome of this prediction has yet to be seen.

THREE FUTURE EVENTS IN MEDJUGORJE

Medjugorje is the single Marian apparition site where Mary speaks the most. Mary says there will be three warning events given to the world, each to be preannounced by Father Petar Liubicic. The first event will be an illumination of conscience, which is seen and felt interiorly by each person in the world. People will see themselves as God sees them—with a focus on the wrong they have done and the good they failed to do. There will be a short period of time for confession and conversion. The second event involves healing miracles. The third event is a visible, indestructible sign on Apparition Hill in Medjugorje placed by Jesus. It will be a supernatural sign for remaining atheists.

The divine warning events will occur during the lifetime of the Medjugorje visionaries, who were born in the 1960s. It is important to note that Father Liubicic, who will announce the events, was born in 1946. This means the three events will occur soon. When the supernatural sign comes, it will be too late for many. Now is the time for the faithful to deepen their own faith and pray for the conversion of nonbelievers.

WORLD CATASTROPHE BY FIRE

In Akita, Japan, Mary warned us of a terrible catastrophe by fire that will be inflicted on a large part of humanity. Fire will fall from the sky, wiping out the good and the bad. The only armaments remaining for survivors will be prayer and the sign left by Mary's Son, Jesus. However, this catastrophe can be mitigated with sufficient prayer, penance, and trust. As more atheists convert to Christianity, the extent of the catastrophe lessens.

THE CATASTROPHE CAN BE MITIGATED OR AVOIDED

In Amsterdam, Mary explained her role in saving the world from catastrophe. She offered a new prayer for the conversion of all nations to share with the faithful worldwide. Mary requested prayer by the faithful for the Holy Spirit to live in the hearts of all nations. She also requested that the Vatican approve the fifth Marian dogma, which is her new vocation as Co-Redemptrix, Mediatrix, and Advocate.

The Vatican has not yet approved her request. In addition, Mary still needs more of the faithful worldwide to pray for the Holy Spirit to live in all nations. Mary needs both requests completed before she can use divine graces and redemption through Christ to save the world from the terrible catastrophe.

During an apparition in San Nicolas, Argentina, it was explained that the mother of Jesus must be accepted to save the world from catastrophe. Jesus chose the heart of his mother. Souls will come to Jesus through the means of her Immaculate Heart.

A TIME OF GRACE

Mary said we live in a time of grace in the early twenty-first century. This time was granted by the Father for humanity to return to God. However, it also allows time for Satan's work to continue. Mary told the visionaries in Medjugorje that this would be the last location for her apparitions. There would no longer be a need for her customary interventions on earth. Ominously, Pope John Paul II said the twenty-first century would be the century of religion—or it would not be at all.

MARY WILL FETTER SATAN INTO THE INFERNAL ABYSS

In Quito, Ecuador, Mary predicted a final resolution to the crisis. However, she never gave a time frame for this resolution. Mary promised that just when it seems all hope is lost, she will intervene and initiate "the happy beginning of the complete restoration. This will mark the arrival of my hour, when I, in a marvelous way, will dethrone the proud and cursed Satan, trampling him under my feet and fettering him in the infernal abyss."

MARY'S CALL TO PRAYER

At a time when most Christians around the globe lack a fidelity to prayer, the mother of Jesus speaks to us. She calls the faithful to pray more, to pray for atheists, to pray for the Holy Spirit to live in the hearts of all nations, to pray for Christian church leaders, to pray fervently, to pray in front of the cross, and to pray every day. Through the Holy Spirit, Christians were given the power of prayer to stop wars and cause natural laws to be suspended. To avoid a worldwide catastrophe by fire that may bring an early end to the twenty-first century, Christians must answer Mary's call to prayer. The power of the Holy Spirit is victorious on earth only when there is fidelity to prayer.

ADDENDUM

MARIAN APPARITION SITES

The Roman Catholic Church or Coptic Orthodox Church approved thirty-four Marian apparition sites as "worthy of belief" at varied levels. Eighteen of those sites were summarized in this book. A comprehensive list of all thirty-four Marian apparition sites is shown below:

1. 40 Apparition in Zaragoza, Spain
2. 1061 Apparition in Walsingham, England
3. 1251 Apparition in Aylesford, England
4. 1490 Apparition in Monte Figogna, Italy
5. 1531 Apparition in Mexico City, Mexico*
6. 1570 Apparition in Tamil Nadu, India
7. 1594 Apparition in Quito, Ecuador*
8. 1608 Apparition in Siluva, Lithuania
9. 1664 Apparition in Saint Etienne-le-Laus, France
10. 1798 Apparition in La Vang, Viet Nam
11. 1830 Apparition in Paris, France*
12. 1842 Apparition in Rome, Italy*
13. 1846 Apparition in La Salette, France*
14. 1858 Apparition in Lourdes, France*
15. 1859 Apparition in Champion, Wisconsin, United States

16. 1871 Apparition in Pontmain, France*
17. 1876 Apparition in Pellevoisin, France
18. 1877 Apparition in Gietrzwald, Poland*
19. 1879 Apparition in Knock, Ireland*
20. 1917 Apparition in Fatima, Portugal*
21. 1932 Apparition in Beauraing, Belgium*
22. 1933 Apparition in Banneux, Belgium
23. 1945 Apparition in Amsterdam, Netherlands*
24. 1947 Apparition in L'lle-Bouchard, France
25. 1948 Apparition in Lipa, Philippines*
26. 1968 Apparition in Zeitoun, Egypt*
27. 1973 Apparition in Akita, Japan*
28. 1980 Apparition in Cuapa, Nicaragua
29. 1981 Apparition in Kibeho, Rwanda*
30. 1981 Apparition in Medjugorje, Bosnia and Herzegovina*
31. 1983 Apparition in San Nicolas, Argentina*
32. 1984 Apparition in Miranda, Venezuela
33. 2000 Apparition in Asyut, Egypt
34. 2009 Apparition in Giza, Egypt

*Denotes apparition sites included in this book.

NOTES

Preface

1 (Catholic authentication of apparitions) www.catholicnews.com. Catholic News Service. "How the church determines a true Marian apparition." Junno Arocho Esteves. April 8, 2017.

2 (Catholic authentication of apparitions) www.catholicnewsagency.com. Catholic News Agency. "Expert explains Church's criteria for confirming Marian apparitions." Salvatore M. Perrella. May 8, 2008.

Chapter 1

1 (Our Lady of Medjugorje) www.medjugorje.com. Caritas of Birmingham, Alabama.

2 (Life after death) www.patheos.com. Patheos. "Medjugorje Visionary 'We are Created for Eternity' Fascinating Insights into Life after Death." Stephen Ryan. January 5, 2018.

Chapter 2

1 (Thomas Aquinas) www.britannica.com. "St. Thomas Aquinas, Italian Christian Theologian and Philosopher." Marie-Dominique Chenu. April 27, 2020.

2 (Jesus speaks of works of the Holy Spirit) *Holy Bible*. The New American Bible. Catholic Bible Press. Nashville. 1987. John 14:11–21. Whoever believes in Jesus will do works greater than he accomplished, with the help of the Holy Spirit.

3 (miracles as evidence of the Holy Spirit) *Holy Bible*. The New American Bible. Catholic Bible Press. Nashville. 1987. Mark 16:9–20. A resurrected

Jesus said to the apostles, "Go into all the world and preach the Gospel to all creation. He who has believed and has been baptized shall be saved; but he who has disbelieved shall be condemned. And these signs will accompany those who have believed … they will lay hands on the sick, and they will recover."

4 (miracles as evidence of the Holy Spirit) *Holy Bible*. The New American Bible. Catholic Bible Press. Nashville. 1987. Acts 15:6–12. Peter stood up and said Gentiles should also hear the Gospel and believe.

5 (healing miracles) *Holy Bible*. The New American Bible. Catholic Bible Press. Nashville. 1987. Matthew 8:6–34. Jesus healed a paralyzed servant and Peter's mother when she was sick. Jesus cast out demons and calmed the seas.

6 (healing miracles) *Holy Bible*. The New American Bible. Catholic Bible Press. Nashville. 1987. Matthew 9:20–34. Jesus healed a blind man and raised a girl from the dead.

7 (healing miracles) *Holy Bible*. The New American Bible. Catholic Bible Press. Nashville. 1987. Matthew 12:13. Jesus healed a man with a withered hand.

8 (healing miracles) *Holy Bible*. The New American Bible. Catholic Bible Press. Nashville. 1987. Matthew 20:30–34. Jesus healed two blind men.

9 (healing miracles) *Holy Bible*. The New American Bible. Catholic Bible Press. Nashville. 1987. Matthew 21:19–20. Jesus withered a fig tree.

10 (Jesus heals blind with mud and water) *Holy Bible*. The New American Bible. Catholic Bible Press. Nashville. 1987. John 9:1–41. Jesus mixes spit and dirt to place mud on a blind man's eyes. He tells the man to go to the pool of Siloam to wash, and his vision returns.

11 (Moses and Elijah apparition) *Holy Bible*. The New American Bible. Catholic Bible Press. Nashville. 1987. Matthew 17:1–9. During the Transfiguration, there were apparitions of Moses and Elijah with Jesus and three apostles.

12 (transfiguration) *Holy Bible*. The New American Bible. Catholic Bible Press. Nashville. 1987. Matthew 17:1–9. God told Peter, James, and John to listen to Jesus.

13 (turning water into wine) *Holy Bible*. The New American Bible. Catholic Bible Press. Nashville. 1987. John 2:1–11. At a wedding where his mother was also in attendance, Jesus performed a miracle by turning water into wine using six stone water pots, each holding thirty gallons.

14 (Pentecost) *Holy Bible*. The New American Bible. Catholic Bible Press. Nashville. 1987. Acts 2:1–41, 3:1–26, 4:1–4.

Chapter 3

1 (Gabriel and Mary) *Holy Bible*. The New American Bible. Catholic Bible Press. Nashville. 1987. Luke 1:32.

2 (Mary says may it be done) *Holy Bible*. The New American Bible. Catholic Bible Press. Nashville. 1987. Luke 1:32.

3 (Word became flesh) *Holy Bible*. The New American Bible. Catholic Bible Press. Nashville. 1987. John 1:14.

4 (Holy House) www.catholicnewsagency.com. Catholic News Agency. "Did angels really carry the Holy House of Mary to Loreto, Italy?" Courtney Mares. December 10, 2018.

5 (Holy House) www.catholicexchange.com. Catholic Exchange. "The Mysterious Holy House of Loreto." K. V. Turley. October 10, 2017.

6 (Loreto) www.catholictradition.org. "The Miracle of Loreto." Lee Wells.

7 (Loreto) www.tfp.org. The American Society for the Defense of Tradition, Family and Property. "Science Confirms: Angels Took the House of Our Lady of Nazareth to Loreto." Luis Dufaur. August 7, 2016.

8 (the Crusades) *Encyclopedia Britannica*. "Crusades." 2017. Religious wars occurred between the Catholic Church and Muslims over control of the Holy Land. There were eight wars between 1096 and 1291.

Chapter 4

1 (honoring Mary) *Beginning Apologetics 6*. Father Frank Chacon and Jim Burnham. San Juan Catholic Seminars. 2000–2012, 12–35. Mary is the mother of God.

2 (honoring Mary) *Holy Bible*. The New American Bible. Catholic Bible Press. Nashville. 1987. Luke 1:26–56. The archangel Gabriel says Mary is filled with the Holy Spirit, calls her blessed.

3 (Hail Mary) *Holy Bible*. The New American Bible. Catholic Bible Press. Nashville. 1987. Luke 1:28. The archangel Gabriel greets Mary with a respectful greeting used for royalty.

4 (Hail Mary) *Holy Bible*. The New American Bible. Catholic Bible Press. Nashville. 1987. Luke 1:39–45. Elizabeth told Mary, "Blessed among women are you, and blessed is the fruit of your womb."

5 (Mary in John's care) *Holy Bible*. The New American Bible. Catholic Bible Press. Nashville. 1987. John 19:26–27.

6 (Queen of Heaven) *Holy Bible*. The New American Bible. Catholic Bible Press. Nashville. 1987. Revelation 12:1.

7 (Mary) Catechism of the Catholic Church. Doubleday, New York. 1994. Paragraph 6.963, 273-276. Mary – Mother of Christ, Mother of the Church.

8 (Hail Mary) My Saint Pio Prayer Book. The Padre Pio Foundation of America. 2018, 7. The Hail Mary prayer is: "Hail Mary, full of grace; the Lord is with thee. Blessed art thou among women, and blessed is the fruit of thy womb, Jesus. Holy Mary, Mother of God, pray for us sinners, now, and at the hour of our death. Amen."

9 (praying the rosary) USCCB.org/how-to-pray-the-rosary. United States Catholic Conference of Bishops, "How to Pray the Rosary."

10 (Glory Be) My Saint Pio Prayer Book. The Padre Pio Foundation of America. 2018, 7.

11 (prayer to Mary) Mother Teresa: A Simple Path. Lucinda Vardey. Ballantine Books. 1995. xxv–xxvi. Mother Teresa and the Missionaries of Charity often prayed to Mary.

Chapter 5

1 (Protestant Reformation) *Encyclopedia Britannica*. "Reformation Christianity." 2017. Luther posted *The Ninety-Five Theses* on October 31, 1517.

2 (Protestant Reformation) Roots of the Reformation. Karl Adam. CH Resources. 2012, 11–41. There was a moral collapse of the popes.

3 (Zwingli) *Funk & Wagnalls New Encyclopedia*. Vol. 28. Funk & Wagnalls Corporation. 1993, 179–80. Huldrych Zwingli developed a separate Protestant group different from Lutheranism. He believed in less control by government over religion.

4 (Anabaptist) *Funk & Wagnalls New Encyclopedia*. Vol. 2. Funk & Wagnalls Corporation. 1993, 99–100. An Anabaptist means one who baptizes again, as an adult.

5 (dual source of revelation) Catechism of the Catholic Church. Doubleday, New York. 1994. Part 1. Section 1. Chapter 2. Article 2.III.84. Catholicism uses both scripture and tradition to determine church doctrine.

6 (early Protestantism) Pew Research Center. Religion & Public Life. Five Centuries after Reformation, Catholic-Protestant Divide in Western Europe Has Faded. August 31, 2017.

7 (remove seven books from the Old Testament) Catholicism and Fundamentalism. Karl Keating. Ignatius Press. 1988, 132. Luther rejected

seven books of the Old Testament because of conflicts with some of his theories, including purgatory.
8 (praying to saints) *Catholic Biblical Apologetics. The Communion of Saints. Praying to the Saints.* Paul Flanagan and Robert Schihl. 1985–2014. Catholics pray to saints in heaven, but they do not worship them.

Chapter 6

1 (Guadalupe) Catholic.org/saints. Catholic Online. 2018. An apparition of Our Lady of Guadalupe occurred in 1531 to Juan Diego.
2 (Guadalupe) CatholicNewsAgency.com/resources/ourladyofguadalupe. Catholic News Agency. The tilma and painting are undeteriorated 470 years later.

Chapter 7

1 (Divine Infant) www.catholicworldreport.com. Catholic World Report. "The 400-year-old Marian apparition that is particularly relevant today." Jim Graves. June 7, 2017.
2 (Divine Infant) www.divinemysteries.info. Divine Mysteries and Miracles. "Our Lady of Good Success, Madrid, Spain / Quito, Ecuador, 1610." John Carpenter. July 17, 2016.
3 (Our Lady of The Good Event) www.crisismagazine.com. "Our Lady of Good Success Speaks to Us Today." Jonathan B. Coe. June 25, 2019.
4 (Our Lady of The Good Event) www.ourladyofgoodsuccess.com. "Our Lady of Good Success."

Chapter 8

1 (Miraculous Medal) www.aleteia.org. Aleteia. "St. Catherine Laboure: The beautiful story of a girl, her mother, and the Miraculous Medal."
2 (Miraculous Medal) www.jesusmariasite.org. Jesus Maria. "Marian Apparitions: Paris 1830 France."

Chapter 9

1 (Our Lady of Zion in Rome) www.stphilipcc.org. St. Philip the Apostle Catholic Church, Lewisville, Texas. "Our Lady of Zion."
2 (Rome) www.marypages.com. "Rome, Italy 1842."

Chapter 10

1 (La Salette) www.catholicstraightanswers.com. Catholic Straight Answers. "What is the story of La Salette?."
2 (La Salette) www.theotokos.org. "La Salette Apparition: September 1946."

Chapter 11

1 (Our Lady of Lourdes) *Bernadette Speaks*. Rene Laurentin. Pauline Books & Media. 2000.
2 (Lourdes) *Funk & Wagnalls New Encyclopedia*, Vol. 16. Funk & Wagnalls Corp. 1993, 239. The first church in Lourdes, France, was built in 1876. A three-story basilica was added in 1889, which holds four thousand people. An underground basilica was added in 1958, holding twenty thousand people, with access to the spring's healing powers.
3 (Lourdes) CatholicNewsAgency.com/resources/ourladyoflourdes. Catholic News Agency. Multiple apparitions of Mary were seen in Lourdes, France.

Chapter 12

1 (Our Lady of Pontmain) www.roman-catholic-saints.com. Roman Catholic Saints. "Our Lady of Pontmain." January 17.
2 (Pontmain) www.catholicstraightanswers.com. Catholic Straight Answers. "What is the story behind our Blessed Mother's title, Our Lady of Hope?."

Chapter 13

1 (Our Lady of Gietrzwald) www.aleteia.org. "Our Lady of Gietrzwald: Poland's only approved Marian appearance." October 18, 2017.
2 (Gietrzwald) www.stphilipcc.org. St. Philip the Apostle Church, Lewisville, Texas. "Our Lady of Gietrzwald."

Chapter 14

1 (Our Lady of Knock) www.knockshrine.ie. Knock Shrine. "The Story of Knock."

2 (Our Lady of Knock) www.catholictraditions.org. Catholic Traditions. "Our Lady of Knock."
3 (Our Lady of Knock) www.aleteia.org. Aleteia. "Who is Our Lady of Knock? The silent apparition." Larry Peterson. June 16, 2018.

Chapter 15

1 (Our Lady of Fatima) _**Fatima in Lucia's own words**_. Sister Maria Lucia. 2018. Sister Lucia's memoirs.
2 (Fatima) www.tfp.org. The American Society for the Defense of Tradition, Family and Property. "Why the Fatima Chastisement and Triumph Await Us." John Horvat II. October 10, 2017.
3 (Fatima) www.fatima.org. Fatima. "Prophesies Already Fulfilled: The Four Chastisements."
4 (Fatima) www.catholicnewsagency.com. "Everything You Need to Know about Fatima." Mary Farrow. May 8, 2017.
5 (Fatima) www.washingtonpost.com. "Our Lady of Fatima: The Virgin Mary promised three kids a miracle that 70,000 gathered to see." Katherine Arcement. October 13, 2017.
6 (World War II) *Encyclopedia Britannica*. "The Blast of World War II."
7 (Russia consecration) www.ewtn.com. "Papal Consecrations to the Immaculate Heart." Pope John Paul II. 1984.
8 (Pope John Paul's homily) www.rosary-center.org. "Pope John Paul II May 13, 1982 homily at Fatima."

Chapter 16

1 (Our Lady of Beauraing) www.ncregister.com. National Catholic Register. "The Golden Heart of Our Lady of Beauraing." Pam Armstrong. August 10, 2016.
2 (Beauraing) www.theotokos.org. "The Apparitions at Beauraing."

Chapter 17

1 (Our Lady of All Nations) www.divinemysteries.info. "Our Lady of All Nations, Amsterdam, Holland, 1945–1959." John Carpenter. August 15, 2016.
2 (Amsterdam) www.marypages.com. Foundation MaryPages. "The Lady of All Nations."

3 (Fifth dogma) www.catholicexchange.com. Catholic Exchange. "Our Lady of All Nations: The Fifth Dogma." Dr. Mark Miravalle and Richard L. Russell. October 21, 2013.

4 (Fifth dogma) www.catholicexchange.com. Catholic Exchange. "Do We Need a New Marian Dogma." October 9, 2019.

Chapter 18

1 (Teresing at age 84) www.all-about-the-virgin-mary.com. "Teresing Castillo, the Lipa Visionary: Sixty-Three Years Later." Virginia G. Guzman-Manzo, MD. 2011.

2 (Our lady of Lipa) www.divinemysteries.info. Divine Mysteries and Miracles. "Mary, Mediatrix of all Grace, Lipa, Philippines, 1948 and 1990." Manuel Lamiroy. August 17, 2016.

Chapter 19

1 (Our Lady of Zeitoun) www.catholicworldreport.com. The Catholic World Report. "Our Lady of Zeitoun and Christianity in Egypt." Filip Mazurczak. April 26, 2017.

2 (Zeitoun) www.aleteia.org. "This Marian apparition in Egypt was witnessed by at least 250,000 people." Philip Kosloski. May 5, 2019.

3 (Zeitoun) www.thechristianreview.com. "When Mary Returned to Egypt: The Apparitions at Zeitoun." Peter LaFave. January 21, 2016.

Chapter 20

1 (Our Lady of Akita) www.ewtn.com. EWTN. "A Message from Our Lady: Akita, Japan." John Ata. November 2011.

2 (Akita) www.aleteia.org. "Our Lady of Akita's powerful message to the world." Philip Kosloski. May 14, 2019.

Chapter 21

1 (Our Lady of Kibeho) *Our Lady of Kibeho*. Immaculee Ilibagiza. Hay House, Inc. 2008.

2 (Our Lady of Kibeho) Website www.divinemysteries.info/our-lady-of-kibeho-rwanda-africa-1981-1989. "Our Lady of Kibeho, Rwanda, Africa, 1981–1989." John Carpenter. September 1, 2016.

3 (Authentication) www.indefenseofthecross.com. In Defense of the Cross. "Kibeho."

4 (Purgatory) *Holy Bible*. The New American Bible. Catholic Bible Press. Nashville. 1987. 2 Maccabees 12:39–46. Judas Maccabeus prayed for God to forgive his dead soldiers and paid money to the church as atonement.

Chapter 22

1 (Medjugorje) www.medjugorje.org. Medjugorje Web. 2020.

2 (Our Lady of Medjugorje) www.medjugorje.com. Caritas of Birmingham, Alabama.

3 (apparitions at Medjugorje) www.catholicnewsagency.com. "The 100-Year Test." Joe Tremblay. February 1, 2013.

4 (Medjugorje miracle) Miracle at Medjugorje. Wayne Weible. 1985.

5 (Garabandal illumination of conscience) www.garabandal.org. The Garabandal Story. Messages from Our Lady of Garabandal.

Chapter 23

1 (Argentina) www.catholicnewsagency.com. Catholic News Agency. "A Marian apparition has been approved in Argentina—and it's a big deal." June 4, 2016.

2 (San Nicolas) www.divinemysteries.info. Divine Mysteries and Miracles. "Our Lady of the Rosary, San Nicolas, Argentina." John Carpenter. September 3, 2016.

3 (San Nicolas) www.cruxnow.com. Crux. "Bishop stops publication of revelations at Argentina Medjugorje." March 18, 2017.

Chapter 24

1 (Pope John Paul II) *John Paul the Great*. Peggy Noonan. Publisher Viking Penguin. 2005.

2 (Pope John Paul II) CBN.com/churchandministry/pope-john-paul-II. Christian Broadcasting Network. 2017. Pope John Paul II canonized more saints than all the popes during the past five hundred years combined.

3 (World Youth Day) worldyouthday.com. 2017. World Youth Day began in 1985 under Pope John Paul II and is held every two or three years in a different city around the world.

4 (number of Christians) Pew Research Center's Forum on Religion & Public Life. Global Christianity. December 19, 2011.

Chapter 25

1 (Our Lady of Medjugorje) www.medjugorje.com. Caritas of Birmingham, Alabama.

2 (Twenty-first century) *Crossing the Threshold of Hope*. His Holiness John Paul II. Copyright 1994. Publisher Alfred A. Knopf, Inc.

Addendum

1 (List of approved Marian apparitions) www.wikipedia.org. List of Marian Apparitions. June 13, 2020.

INDEX

T

U

V

Z